# Gifts of Gold

AN APPLES OF GOLD RESOURCE

# Gifts of Gold

## Gathering, Training, and Encouraging Mentors

# Betty Huizenga

For Her. For God. For Real.
faithfulwoman.com

Faithful Woman is an imprint of
Cook Communications Ministries, Colorado Springs, Colorado 80918
Cook Communications, Paris, Ontario
Kingsway Communications, Eastbourne, England

GIFTS OF GOLD
© 2002 by Betty Huizenga. All rights reserved.

Printed in the United States of America.

1 2 3 4 5 6 7 8 9 10 Printing/Year 06 05 04 03 02

Senior Editor: Janet Lee
Cover design: Andrea L. Boven / Boven Design Studio, Inc.


Library of Congress Cataloging-in-Publication Data

Huizenga, Betty.
  Gifts of gold : gathering, training, and encouraging mentors : an
Apples of Gold resource / Betty Huizenga.
     p. cm.
  ISBN 0-7814-3809-8
  1. Church work with women. 2. Mentoring in church work. I. Title.
  BV4445 .H85 2002
  253'.7--dc21
                            200200033

Apples of Gold mentors are making a difference—one life at a time. Here are some of the comments made by young women in the program:

"The best part of the program for me was the mentors and all the sharing that was done. I love the wisdom from the mentors and what they have to offer—knowledge, compassion and a warm hug. I couldn't wait for Wednesday to roll around—loved it all!"

"It was incredible to be on the receiving end of the mentor's generosity. To think they would put so much time, energy and some dollars into investing in our lives touched my heart deeply. They are wise, humble, open and honest and very genuine."

"The best part of the program was being able to interact with these godly mentors on a personal level. I treasured the time with them and listened expectantly for whatever any of them had to say. Also—the wonderful mix of beautiful table settings, the fabulous food, resources, tips, book recommendations, HUGS, and the way God spoke to my heart through the lessons—in other words, everything!"

"The whole program was fabulous. The Bible and cooking lessons were so helpful and inspiring. However, the best part for me was the wisdom and sharing from the mentors. I felt that I couldn't write fast enough to get it all down. I also loved how nurtured I felt every time."

"For me, the entire program was such a fabulous, pampering treat! However, I'd have to say the best part was meeting all of the mentors. To spend time with all of you who have so obviously, so lovingly, so unselfishly dedicated your lives to the Lord and to His service, was the greatest gift to me. Every mentor was so willing to openly share the highs and lows, the good times and struggles of living in God's Word."

"As a new Christian who struggles daily with changing my life so that I am living His word obediently, this was extremely refreshing. I now know that I am not alone in my journey. To all of you, thank you for your devotion and time to this program. Because of all of you, my faith has been strengthened immensely. May God bless all of you."

"I was so blessed to be a part of this ministry. My husband often says how he feels blessed because of the encouragement it brought to me. Thanks for listening to the Lord."

"My prayer for you is that the Lord would continue to use Apples of Gold for women such as myself who need a mentoring program that's so well rounded to remind us of God's design and desire for wives and mothers."

# Dedication

*Gifts of Gold* is written for all the lovely "Golden Women"
of Apples of Gold, A Nurturing Program for Women

# Contents

**Chapter 1—**

## CATCHING THE VISION                    17

*Words of Encouragement*

*The Heart of Apples of Gold*


**Chapter 2—**

## MEANT TO MENTOR                        25

*Your Heritage*

*What is a Mentor?*

*Why Mentor?*

*The Titus 2 Principle*

*Are You a Golden Woman?*


**Chapter 3—**

## READY, SET, NURTURE                    39

*Getting Started*

*Location, Location, Location*

*Child Care*

*Budget Ideas*

*Leadership*

*Bringing Leaders Together*

*Stick to the Plan*

*Starting Right*

*A Time and Place for Everything*

*Quick Tips for Mentors*

*What One Lesson Looks Like*

*Wrapping Things Up*

**Chapter 4—**

**THE COOKING MENTOR**                              **59**

*The Importance of Hospitality*

*An Heirloom Opportunity*

*Teachable Moments*

*Welcome to Apples of Gold*

*The Joy of Cooking*

*Responsibility of the Cooking Mentor*

*Planning the Menu*

*Choosing Recipes*

*Techniques to Demonstrate*

*The Day of Class*

*Kitchen Cleanliness*

*Suggesting Cookbooks and Recipes*

*The Finer Things*

*Family or Guest*

*Cooking Budget*

*Decorating Ideas*

*Options, Options*

*Chapter 5—*

## THE CELEBRATION DINNER 87

*Why Celebrate?*

*Setting the Tables*

*What to Expect*

*Cooking the Dinner*

*A Typical Schedule for Food Preparation*

*Serving the Dinner*

*Food for the Soul*


*Chapter 6—*

## WHAT'S NEXT? 103

*Applesauce—A Wonderful Blend*

*Spring Luncheon*

*Christmas Coffee*

*Topical Studies*

*Appleseeds and Apple Blossoms*

*Final Words*

# *Acknowledgments*

Thanks to the Most High God for initiating this plan in Titus 2 and then inspiring the plan for Apples of Gold in this servant's heart. It is the adventure of a lifetime and joy beyond measure.

I thank Cook Communications for publishing Apples of Gold, and Gifts of Gold, and for believing in this unique and growing ministry to young women around the world.

Janet Lee, Senior Editor at Cook and Editor for Gifts of Gold, has taken the words of this book and ordered them in a way that will help you better understand and enjoy them. Thanks, Janet, for your loving and kind spirit and for the encouragement you are to my heart.

I thank Focus on the Family and the ministry of Renewing the Heart for bringing the ministry of Apples of Gold to women around the world. God has used these Focus ministries to bless this ministry far beyond anything I could ever imagine. What a blessing Focus on the Family is to the people of God! The hopes and dreams of women in South Africa is much the same as those in America and other countries.

It would be impossible to perpetuate this program without the loving and obedient mentors of Apples of Gold. Your enthusiasm and love for the young women in your churches has blessed young hearts and showed them an example to follow. Though I have either written or spoken to many of you, I have not met most of you. Yet, I pray faithfully for you and long to meet you one day. We do have a common interest and bond because of Apples of Gold. Thank you for your service to Christ.

Finally, I must again thank the mentors in the class in which I serve in Holland. They have been such faithful partners. The young women in our classes are so blest to know them and call them friend. These women are most precious to me and I thank each of them: Carol Berens, Mary De Witt, Dee Horne, Jinny Nash, Ruth Slenk, Linda Topp and Irene Zoodsma. You're the best!

# Young at Heart

If you're among the young at heart,
there's work for you to do;
No time to waste—
the younger generation's calling you.
They seek and need your loving care,
advice and wisdom too,
because your hair is turning gray,
they'll listen well to you.

I pulled the covers higher,
and snuggled in my bed.
This time is mine, for things I like,
and books I haven't read.
I've worked so hard these many years,
as you can understand;
This time is now for me, Lord,
for long walks on the sand.

The kids are grown, my time's my own—
I've earned it fair and square.
and now I hear you calling me
Your kingdom's work to share?

And then because I love you, Lord,
I read Your Word and see
that never do You rest or sleep
and how You care for me.
I also read Your words that say,
"If you love Me, you'll obey."
And, in pain I realize
I've followed my own way.


So eagerly I'll follow, Lord.
Give me strength each day;
Give me wisdom, kindness, love.
Teach me what to say.
Help me pass the joy I've found
to those who follow after,
that they may learn to fill their lives
with joy and love and laughter.

And as I watch them grow in You
my spirit will revive;
And every day I'll thank You, Lord,
for keeping me alive.

**BETTY HUIZENGA**
**COPYRIGHT 2000**

# CHAPTER 1

# Catching the Vision

## WORDS OF ENCOURAGEMENT

Since the publishing of the book, *Apples of Gold*, in March of 2000, classes have started all over **this land** and in other countries of the world. It seems that for every class that starts there are new ideas and questions that need to be addressed. For this reason, we are offering this book to encourage the leaders of the program and to share some of the wonderful and encouraging ideas other class leaders have used to enhance their classes. We are indeed learning from one another and growing together.

I have made so many new friends through the Apples of Gold ministry. The website **applesofgold.org** introduces me to new women and classes literally every day. What a joy and blessing to hear from you and receive ideas and encouragement from you. Some of those ideas are shared on the website. We want Apples of Gold to honor God and that happens best as we listen to Him and to one another.

I have also met many of you through my travels and speaking about Apples of Gold at various meetings and churches. Visiting classes is the best! Seeing firsthand how other classes are setting up their meetings, decorating their tables, and meeting the personal needs of each woman is a continuing education for me.

I'm sure many of you have read *The Prayer of Jabez* by Dr. Bruce Wilkerson. That little book has touched the hearts of many people, including mine. The prayer, found in 1 Chronicles 4:9-10, says,

> *Jabez was more honorable than his brothers. His mother had named him Jabez, saying " I gave birth to him in pain". Jabez cried out to the God of Israel, "Oh, that you would bless me and enlarge my territory. Let your hand be with me and keep me from harm so that I will be free from pain. And God granted his request.*

Jabez wanted to rise above the circumstances of his birth. He wisely goes directly to the Lord and asks the Lord to help him. The fact that God granted his request indicates that Jabez asked with the proper motives.

Few of us are in the habit of asking God to bless us. It is far easier to ask the Lord to bless our family and friends. But asking to be blessed in order to bless others is an unselfish and God-honoring request. I do want that. I want to make a difference in the lives of those around me. I don't want my past, my failures, or my indifference to hinder my work in God's kingdom.

It is such a joy to be reminded of the faithfulness of God. He has 'enlarged the territory' of Apples of Gold in ways I never dreamed. Women are gravitating to this ministry because it meets a deep need in their hearts and lives. The testimonies of those who have been touched, some of which you will read in this book, bear witness to how God is working. Even so, sometimes I struggle with feelings of inadequacy. Perhaps you can relate to the following illustration:

In Florida, there is an exterminating company that uses a unique way of advertising. They have VW bugs with mouse ears on top and a long tail behind. One day as I was following one of these adorable cars, I realized that as the car sped along, the mouse ears flopped back and flattened out—not at all the proper position for listening. Sometimes, I am going so fast that my ears cannot hear. I need to stop and be quiet in order to hear the voice of God.

It had been a difficult couple of weeks. I was facing some struggles and I was discouraged. I asked the Lord to remind me of His call and to encourage my heart. On this particular restless night, the Spirit of

God spoke to my heart. God gave me a wonderful time in His presence. I'm not sure why these times seem to come at night, except that night-time is one of the rare times I am quiet and still. In fact, every song I have written has come to me in the night hours.

Earlier that week, I had written:

> Life is really hard today.
> I don't know what to think or say.
> I even stumble when I pray.
> Life is really hard today.
>
> But Lord I know if I am still
> And listen to Your tender voice,
> You will help me know Your will.
> My heart will once again rejoice.
>
> And sure enough Lord, You came through
> With help and wisdom, tried and true.
> With love of friends and many prayers
> You showed exactly what to do.
>
> For love, so generous, so undeserved,
> My grateful heart can now rejoice.
> Thank you for reminding me
> To listen to Your tender voice.

During this sleepless night as I listened to God, He reminded me, "I am faithful".

My mind was flooded with His presence as He took me down the path of my life starting 32 years before when I committed my life to Him in Annapolis, Maryland.

There is a song I love which I heard many years ago. It is not a familiar song, but it is a wonderful song.

## THOSE QUIET TIMES

**WORDS BY H.B. BARTON          MUSIC BY ROBERT BROOKS**

Those quiet times I thank Thee for, when I commune with Thee;
And in Thy presence peace I find, when Thou dost speak to me.
Those silent moments in the night, when sleep has passed me by,
My thoughts all dwell with Thee, as Thou dost draw me nigh.
How precious are those quiet times when Thy peace fills my soul,
And all my sorrows from me flee, and Thou dost make me whole.

O Lord how precious is the plan thy grace provides for man;
If we but stop and rest with Thee, we are renewed again.
So bid my soul in peace to rest with Thee, O Lord, I pray,
When weary, tired and worn, I stumble on my way.
Those quiet times are blest to me, for in them flies my goal
To walk with Thee, my Lord and King, and find peace for my soul.

It is in those quiet times that God reminds me of all the precious friends He has put in my life—to mentor, to guide, to bring me to where I am today. All of us can point to dear people God has brought into our lives—those who love, confront, and urge us on to reach the highest goal to which God has called us. Now it is our turn—yours and mine—to give back to others what we have received.

This excites me. It reminds me of the original call of God to start Apples of Gold. Listening to His voice and following His path brings a joy that we could never have on our own. In Matthew 6:33, my husband's favorite verse, we read, "Seek first the kingdom of God and His right-eousness, and all these things will be added unto you."

You who are mentors in Apples of Gold are wonderful new friends to me—*gifts of gold* from the Lord's own hand. You are part of that train of friends God is using to grow my spiritual life to follow His purpose.

I am so thankful for each of you. I pray for you often, even for those of you I have never met. I pray that your life will be a blessing to the young women God puts into your path, and that you will receive a blessing, greater than you can imagine, for your obedience.

## THE HEART OF APPLES OF GOLD

The title for the book, *Apples of Gold,* is taken from <u>Proverbs 25:11.</u> "A word fitly spoken is like apples of gold in a setting of silver."

Picture ripe, golden apples, polished to a luster, artistically arranged in the finest sterling bowl, or a 24-karat gold inlay of apples on an exquisite silver platter. This word picture highlights again the beauty and value of wise words spoken at the right time. The wise teachers of Proverbs don't consider it hyperbole to aim to make one's speech a work of art.

Apples of Gold is such a fitting title for this nurturing program. This is a program that combines the study of scripture with bringing that scripture to life everyday by the way we show kindness, love for our family, submission to God and others, purity of body and spirit, and genuine hospitality to those around us. These are the areas mentioned in Titus 2 and upon which the Apples of Gold ministry rests.

### APPLES OF GOLD MISSION STATEMENT

The primary purpose of Apples of Gold is for older women to nurture younger women in the Word of God, the Bible, and to encourage them to obey that Word.

The secondary purpose of the program is the practical application of these principles:

#### Cooking skills

Each week the first hour is held in the kitchen, learning about menu planning, and cooking wonderful food for our families. If more families eat together around the table sharing not only food, but devotions, and encouraging conversation, our families will grow together and in Christ.

#### Relational skills

We want to build friendships among women and between generations. By learning to understand and love one another, we help to build the church at large. We can't understand one another without knowing one another. Apples of Gold is a bridge—building ministry between older and younger.

### Homemaking skills

Many young women today have not been taught such simple tasks as setting the table properly, or proper etiquette. Having an understanding of these skills will help these young women to feel more confident and aid them in passing these skills along to their children.

### Hospitality

Sharing hospitality with family, friends and even strangers, is one of the great pleasures of life. Yet, today, it is nearly a lost art. We are more and more pre-occupied with our homes, yet use them less to warm the hearts of our friends and entertain strangers. Apples of Gold seeks to encourage women "they can do it" and we teach by example.

The program is based on the principles found in Titus 2:3-5, which teach how to enhance our spiritual and personal lives, the lives of our families and the lives of those around us.

Titus 2:3-5 states,

> *Likewise, teach the older women to be reverent in the way they live, not to be slanderers or addicted to much wine, but to teach what is good.*
>
> *Then they can train the younger women to love their husbands and children, to be self-controlled and pure, to be busy at home, to be kind and to be subject to their husbands, so that no one will malign the word of God.*

In these verses, Paul highlights the value of a woman's influence and work. Whether young or old, a woman has the potential to affect her world by her character and the conduct of her life.

Some have seen these verses as a restriction on a woman's role, but they are not. Instead, these verses point to the tremendous opportunities available to a creative, godly woman who purposes to build a life where love and faith can flourish.

As responsibilities at home decrease with time a woman is able to use the character and wisdom she has gained to have a broader influence on the world. It is important to note that her impact comes primarily through her godly character, not through the accomplishments of domestic or professional duties.

I especially like the word nurture for describing this ministry. The word nurture means to nourish and rear. Nurturing indicates active participation. In Apples of Gold, we nourish both body and spirit. Nourish means to foster or cherish. So we both nourish and cherish one another. I love that. It is meaningful, it is loving, it is fulfilling.

Many classes ask the younger women to fill in an evaluation sheet at the conclusion of their 6 weeks together. These evaluations are a joy to read and I will share from some of them throughout this book. Here's an example:

> **This program has impacted every part of my life! God's timing was perfect in placing Apples of Gold in my life this summer. The encouragement, love and teaching in each area of the study that I received was such a blessing. I have such hope now that I can be the woman God wants me to be and live a victorious life by His strength. You are all wonderful examples to me.**

At the heart of Apples of Gold is the desire to touch the lives of women like this one. It doesn't take a college degree or seminary training. All you need is a heart willing to serve and share what God has taught you during your life journey.

# CHAPTER 2

# Meant to Mentor

## YOUR HERITAGE

A heritage is not a heritage unless it is passed on from one generation to another. The work of God in your life has left you with a wealth of knowledge and experience—a treasured heirloom just waiting to be passed along.

Each of you probably has an heirloom at home, a part of your heritage handed down to you or something you plan to give to your children one day. I still wrap up in a blanket given to me by my Grammy for a wedding gift. There is no longer a silky edge, but it still gives warmth and comfort to my body and to my heart.

Each of our children has a baby blanket knitted for them by my mom. She knitted 17 of the same white blanket, one for each grandchild. I treasure the blanket that was in her knitting basket when she died. She never gave up and always gave her heart to her children and grandchildren.

One of our most treasured heirlooms is certainly the Word of God. Second Timothy 3:16-17 reminds us:

> *All scripture is God-breathed (or inspired by God) and is useful for teaching, rebuking, correcting and training in righteousness, so that the man of God may be thoroughly equipped for every good work.*

How precious it is to have God's words written down for us through all these generations. They guide, comfort, and teach us about God the Father, Jesus Christ, our Redeemer, and the Holy Spirit, our Comforter and Teacher.

There are certain qualities about heirlooms that are much like us:

- **An heirloom has a story that goes with it.**
  God has written for each of us a story that accompanies our life.
- **An heirloom brings delight to its owner.**
  God wants us to delight in the spiritual heritage we have in Him and to understand His delight in us, whatever our story.
- **An heirloom is meant to be preserved and passed on from generation to generation.**
  God has promised to keep us to the end and pass on our faith to other generations.

Nurturing others is much like passing on a priceless heirloom. Nurturing is passing wisdom, ideas and the truths of God's Word from one generation to the next. Sharing ideas from life lessons is a forgotten art. We have neglected it and in the process, lost the joy and sheer fun of days gone by.

I so clearly remember when my mom's sisters gathered to can and freeze foods, to mend clothing over a cup of coffee and what laughter and fun they had in the process.

My precious sister-in-law, Jeanne, taught me how to can peaches and pickles. Her five children and our four were underfoot, but we had great satisfaction in working together and lining up the jars as they came out of the canner.

The times when we canned or baked together drew us close. I never had a sister so it was Jeanne who taught me so much about being a wife and mom. When she died at the age of 36, it put a hole in my heart that has never been filled by anyone else. What she taught me was just for us!

What happened between Jeanne and me was extraordinary precisely because we were ordinary women who cared for each other. I am ever more aware that God chooses to use people just like you and me to do His extraordinary work. Apples of Gold is the story of how God chose to use an ordinary woman—a wife, mother, and grandmother, to accomplish His purpose. It is for me an act of obedience to a call from God. It does not come from a heart full of self-confidence, but of confidence in an Almighty God.

Apples of Gold is a program that can help you be a "Jeanne" to a young woman who needs a friend to listen—someone to teach her biblical principles and practical skills. Or, someone to just laugh with over a cup of tea.

## WHAT IS A MENTOR?

If you have never had a mentor, you may not be clear on what is expected in a mentoring role. You may feel you can't possibly be a mentor because you don't know what a mentor is?

Bobb Biehl, in his excellent book *Mentoring*, shares his thoughts on the ideal mentor:

- The ideal mentor is honest with you.
- The ideal mentor is a model for you.
- The ideal mentor is deeply committed to you.
- The ideal mentor is open and transparent.
- The ideal mentor is a teacher.
- The ideal mentor believes in your potential.
- The ideal mentor helps you define your dreams.
- The ideal mentor is successful in your eyes, someone you would like to be like.
- The ideal mentor is open to learning from you as well as teaching you.

A trusted friend is a good description for a mentor. There must be a confidence in our relationships with the younger women, a trust that our sharing is sacred. Trust is built week by week as you meet together, laugh and learn together.

Another aspect of mentoring is that of a respected coach. A coach tells you what to do and how to do it but also shows you what and how. Good coaches inspire you by example. This is the type of teaching and training seen in Titus 2. Both the friend and the coach are necessary parts of the mentoring relationship.

My friend Marilyn asks these questions when gathering mentors for a class:

- Can you be a friend?
- Can you listen?
- Can you share what Christ has done in your life?
- Do you care about the needs of other women?
- Do you have a tender heart toward God and others?
  THEN YOU CAN BE A NURTURING WOMAN!

Some of you are already involved in nurturing other women. You have discovered that it takes time and discernment. It also takes a big heart. Mostly it takes a big heart!

A good mentor can discern whether a young woman needs additional time to share after class. We need to get to know the women well enough to feel the needs of their hearts and then seek to attend to those needs.

We need to be good listeners. It is important that each woman has the opportunity to express her needs and ideas. We need to listen first, then give helpful advice when we can. If we are too quick to give our opinion on a topic, the younger women may be intimidated by our comments and think their ideas are not significant. Be sensitive, gentle, and loving.

A woman who mentors must also have the heart of a servant. She must desire to serve others more than be served. Serving others brings joy to those we serve and to our own heart. It is easy to become selfish and desire to have others serve us. We can become concerned with our own rights and beliefs and not develop a heart of service to others, but once again, we miss the blessing. We need God's help for that. Consider Romans 12:1-2:

*Therefore, I urge you, brothers, in view of God's mercy,*
*to offer your bodies as living sacrifices, holy and pleasing to*
*God—this is your spiritual act of worship. Do not conform*
*any longer to the pattern of this world, but be transformed by the*
*renewing of your mind. Then you will be able to test and*
*approve what God's will is—his good, pleasing and perfect will.*

This example of serving is not wasted on the young women involved in the program, as demonstrated in this testimony I received from an Apples of Gold participant:

**Thank you for the wonderful time I had as part of the Apples of Gold class. The fellowship with other women of all ages, the talk centered on God's Word (instead of just surface talk), and the fun of cooking and feasting on all the delicacies! What a delight!! The mentors exemplified servanthood. What a blessing for young women to experience.**

A mentor should have a cheerful countenance and a Spirit of joy in her life. Psalm 37:4 says, "Delight in the Lord your God and he will give you the desire of your heart." This is a conditional verse—IF we delight, then He will give.

Sometimes we don't really know the desires of our heart. We may think it is a material possession, a new house or car. It may be health or peace of mind. God, however, knows exactly what our heart needs. While thinking about this verse one night, the Lord gave me this little chorus:

Delight in the Lord your God,
The desires of your heart He will give you.
Delight in the Lord your God,
The desires of your heart you will know.
He will give you love beyond measure.
He will give you life that never ends.

Graciously impart,
Peace within your heart,
He will be your faithful friend.
Delight in the Lord your God,
The desires of your heart He will give you.
Delight in the Lord your God
The desires of your heart you will know.

God has shown me that one of the desires of my heart is ministering to young women through Apples of Gold. This ministry has brought such joy and delight to my heart—I pray it will do the same for you.

## WHY MENTOR?

The main reason to mentor is because God calls us to do it. God knows that it is important to mentor, that mentoring has the potential to change lives, and that young women need the wisdom and fellowship of older women. Older women, in turn, are blessed and learn from the lives of the younger women. Often the younger woman becomes the teacher as she challenges us with questions and ideas new to us.

When Mary found out she was going to be the mother of Jesus, she went to visit her relative Elizabeth, an older woman who was also expecting. Mary spent three months with her. I imagine they had many long talks about the childbearing, parenting, and God's work in their lives. Elizabeth could give a different perspective to the younger Mary while Mary's faith and enthusiasm no doubt energized Elizabeth.

Elizabeth and Mary, though different in age, respected the unique work of God in the life of the other. Elizabeth, hearing Mary's greeting and being filled with the Holy Spirit, said, "Blessed are you among women, and blessed is the child you will bear." She was so honored that Mary had come to her home.

Think of young Mary and the incredible circumstances of her pregnancy. Yet she was filled with joy, saying "My soul glorifies the Lord and my spirit rejoices in God my Savior." What an inspiration these two women were to one another!

Such blessings await us if we are open to the Holy Spirit and obedient to His call on our lives. Mentoring brings joy and encouragement to life, both to the older and the younger.

The letters and e-mails that I receive tell me that there are thousands of young women longing to have an older, wiser woman in their lives. Many write that they have prayed for a mentor. Others say they have asked an older woman in their church to mentor them, only to be refused.

Often these young women do not live near their moms. Or they do not have the kind of relationship with their mom that would allow them to discuss a topic like Submission or Purity with her.

You can make a difference in a young woman's life. Your experiences with raising your children, working out the difficulties in your marriage, showing kindness and hospitality to others are a heritage waiting to be passed on to another generation.

Did you ever have a mentor? What difference did it make in your life? If you didn't have a mentor, how would your life be different if you had had someone to talk things over with when you were a young wife and mother.

And what a difference mentoring can make to you! These young women are vital, full of fun and full of hope. They can inspire your life. They can help you to understand your own grown children as you seek solutions together. The friendships I have with these dear women renew my mind. I learn new things by listening to how they think and feel. The issues they face may be the same as those we faced, but because today's world is so totally different than when our children were young, there are new lessons to be learned even for us.

When God calls us, we have a decision to make—to obey or not to obey. There are no other options. Deuteronomy 28: 1-14 talks about the blessings of obedience in different areas of our life. God promises to honor our obedience by blessing our city and country, our family, our crops, and livestock. He says, "Your basket and your kneading bowl will be blessed"(Deuteronomy 28:5). I love to use that verse when I am making bread in class. Isn't it wonderful to know that God cares about every part of our life?

I have also learned that I would rather have the blessing of God through obedience to Him, than the pain of separation from Him through my disobedience. Consider these Bible verses as you think about obedience to God:

> *If you love me, keep my commandments. John 14:15*
> *Obey them not only to win their favor when their eye is on you, but like slaves of Christ, doing the will of God from your heart. Ephesians 6:6*
> *...and receive from him anything we ask, because we obey his commands and do what pleases him. 1 John 3:22*
> *Those who obey his commands live in him, and he in them. And this is how we know that he lives in us: We know it by the Spirit he gave us. 1 John 3:24*
> *This is love for God: to obey his commands. And his commands are not burdensome...1 John 5:3*

In addition to obeying the Lord, there is the blessing of fruit for your labor. What a blessing to watch the young women grow in Christ, to share in their lives, and to know that you are making a difference. Listen to this young woman's words:

**Apples of Gold was soooooo special. I felt like I won a prize to be able to be in it. At Karen's house during the cooking class, I was so overwhelmed with joy I got tears in my eyes (thankfully no one saw). Evie Young stole my heart as she showed us her bread making.**

**I appreciated these mentor women and the whole program. I felt God's love poured out to me through it. Just starting out each time receiving hugs set the tone.**

**It was incredible to be on the receiving end of the mentor's generosity. To think they would put so much time, energy and some dollars into investing in our lives touched my heart deeply. They are wise, humble, open and honest and very genuine.**

**The meetings were a wonderful mix—being spoiled**

**rotten and being challenged to the core. In the lessons we examined different areas of our lives according to the choices God wants for us.**

**The lesson that hit hardest for me was the one on loving your husband. I've made the mistake of being a mom first for too many years. Thank you, Carol, for the wonderful book.**

**I'm inspired to work on other things and plan to keep going back through the book even if it's just to read the scripture verses (I used a pretty colored gel pen to write the verses in those boxes).**

**It's with a grateful heart I tell you mentors I'd like to be just like all of you when I grow up.**

So, why mentor? Why not! It's God's plan, you will be blessed, and you can make a difference. For where your heart is, there is your treasure also.

## THE TITUS 2 PRINCIPLE

God's plan in Titus 2:3-5 is for all women everywhere. Given the changes in our culture—loss of community and extended family, high mobility, fast-paced living—this passage may be even more pertinent today than when it was written. If left to ourselves, we can easily get discouraged. But when someone stands beside us, showing us how, and seasoning the teaching with encouraging words, it makes all the difference in the world.

The Titus 2 passage about mentoring is not an option. God says clearly that the older women are to teach and train the younger women. Those of us who have joined hands and hearts through Apples of Gold are learning that this ministry is important and helpful. God knew that and called us to it.

Note that we are to teach and train. In Apples of Gold, we not only teach through our study of the Bible, but we train by giving practical applications for our lives.

Though at the start I had no bigger dream for Apples of Gold than to minister to the young women in my own church, I now have a passion to see it expand its boundaries. God is using this program to help women grow in Christ and, in the process, strengthen families. We are seeing that the heart needs of women everywhere are similar, and that the Word of God ministers to each heart in a personal way.

The principles in Titus 2 are so important and work together to build our homes and families to the glory of God.

- By loving our husband and children and maintaining self-control (or as one Bible version says, remaining "chaste" or "pure"), we protect our marriages, our children, and our testimony to others.
- When we learn to submit in love to God first, and then to others, loving one another as Christ loves us, we help to bring peace into our homes.
- Our acts of kindness can help change our families, our churches, our neighborhoods, and towns.
- And finally, when we show hospitality to strangers and friends alike, we are showing them what Christ is like.

Another reason I believe God initiated this idea in Titus is to develop friendships among older and older, younger and younger, and older and younger—friendships that are lasting, meaningful and joyous. One of the most common themes of letters I receive from younger women is that they cannot find older women willing to give time and consideration to their needs. Some write that they have prayed for years for a nurturing woman to guide them and be their friend. I have yet to hear from a younger woman who did not want a friend from God in her life!

I also receive much mail from mentors who say that the blessing of Apples of Gold is truly theirs. This is a reciprocal ministry. Mentors find new purpose in their lives as they share with other women the lessons they have learned in their Christian walk. God has planned your life so that you may continue to grow and bear fruit.

*The righteous will flourish like a palm tree, they will grow like a cedar of Lebanon; planted in the house of the Lord, they will flourish in the courts of our God. They will still bear fruit in old age, they will stay fresh and green, proclaiming, the Lord is upright; He is my Rock, and there is no wickedness in Him. Psalm 92: 12-15*

## ARE YOU A GOLDEN WOMAN?

Is God calling you to participate in the life of a young woman or in the ministry of Apples of Gold? If He is, there are some special requirements for that service.

First Timothy 2:9 advises women to dress modestly, with decency and propriety, not with braided hair or gold or pearls or expensive clothes, but with good deeds, appropriate for women who profess to worship God. Our physical appearance is a window to our hearts. Both our dress and our countenance need to be under the control of the Holy Spirit's guidance.

Second Timothy 2:15 reminds us, "do your best to present yourself to God as one approved, a workman who does not need to be ashamed and who correctly handles the word of truth. Avoid godless chatter, because those who indulge in it will become more and more ungodly."

It is important that we handle the words of the Bible with accuracy. This means not giving our own interpretation of that scripture, but to be sure of the meaning and intent of the verse. If a question is asked, and you are unsure of the correct answer, it is better to say you will check and return the right answer next time, than to give the incorrect answer.

Likewise, our words and opinions need to conform to the whole counsel of God's Word. It is easy to slip into the trap of giving our own opinions as God's truth, whether they are or not!

The first verses of Titus 2 give some good advice to us about the qualifications of leadership. "Likewise, teach the older women to be reverent in the way they live, not to be slanderers or addicted to much wine, but to teach what is good." It goes on to say "THEN, they can train the younger women.

The older women should be examples to the younger women, someone to look up to and admire. Then the younger women will listen with respect. Did you notice that the primary qualifications are that the mentor be older and admirable? The passage does not say expert or authority.

Paul understood the responsibility of an elder as an example to other believers. To the believers in Corinth, he writes, "We put no stumbling blocks in anyone's path, so that our ministry will not be discredited…" (2 Corinthians 6:3); "Since we have these promises, dear friends, let us purify ourselves from everything that contaminates body and spirit, perfecting holiness out of reverence for God" (2 Corinthians 7:1).

We need to determine what these stumbling blocks could be for our particular group, and determine not to hinder the gospel of Christ. We need to be aware of things that contaminate our body and spirit and not have any part of them. We need to seek a holy heart!

The woman described in Proverbs 31:10-31 is a woman to emulate—one who brings honor to the name of the Lord and who is fit to serve others because of her character. These qualities are not just for mentoring women but for all women. They are qualities we need to seek after. But nowhere does it say that we can do all this perfectly.

If you have a strong desire to obey the Word of God, to follow Christ as your Lord and Master, seek the Holy Spirit to guide your life, and want to serve in the kingdom, you will make a wonderful friend and mentor to a younger woman. There will be times when you make mistakes, say the wrong thing, or hurt someone's feelings. We all do! Then you can ask for forgiveness and go one from there.

If you feel inadequate to be a leader in Apples of Gold, you are not alone. In Exodus 4:10-17 Moses argues with God about speaking for Him. He says he is not eloquent, and is slow of speech and tongue. God reminds Moses that He created his mouth and will give him words to speak if he will just obey.

Could it be that God is calling you to carry out this mandate of Titus 2? He will guide and direct you as You seek His will for you. If He is calling you, He will help you and teach you so you will be a blessing to these precious younger women.

> *Teach me, O Lord, to follow Your decrees; then I will keep them to the end. Give me understanding, and I will keep your law and obey it with all my heart. Direct me in the path of Your commands, for there I find delight. Psalm 119:33*

# CHAPTER 3

# Ready, Set, Nurture

## GETTING STARTED

Apples of Gold is a fairly easy program to develop. Having said that, I
believe that anything done in Christ's name should be done to the best
of our ability. It takes devoted women who desire to follow the Word
of God, and some good organization. This is most true for a class start.
After the first class, most of the master planning is complete, and following classes will have a good pattern.

There is not one perfect way to do a class, but there are guidelines that
make the class "click". When the leadership remains the same from class
to class, you begin to work as a team. You will begin to sense in each
class where you are most needed, how you can help on a particular day,
and how to pray for your class and its leaders.

As with all good Christ-centered programs, we need to begin with
prayer. We need to pray that we follow God's will for the class, for just
the right leadership, for a home in which to meet, to establish a budget, to decide how to start the class and whom to invite to the first class.

You will need to decide on a day and time. Will this be a weekday class
with a luncheon, or an evening class so working women can attend?
Would a Saturday class work better? You may want to survey the
interested women to see what works best for them. Many churches alter-
nate and have both a weekday and an evening or Saturday class. Our
church has a Wednesday evening class. While the family is at church,

mom is at her class. You will want to meet the needs of the majority of women in your church.

How will you choose the participants for your first class? It is a difficult question. There is a fairness issue. You will most likely have more women interested in participating than your class can handle. I suggest that you make an announcement about Apples of Gold, and hold a special meeting telling what it is about. Tell when the first class is starting, what the requirements are for attendance, and that the first 12 (or your number) to sign up will be in the first class.

## LOCATION, LOCATION, LOCATION

You may already have a home in which to meet. If not, that is the next priority. Be sure the home is a place where the women will feel welcome to kick back and be themselves. If you want the sharing to be real and from the heart, then the setting needs to encourage it. A beautifully decorated home can be a treat if the heart of the home is a welcoming one. In the same way, a modestly furnished home can present a practical lesson in hospitality that every participant can emulate.

Strive to make the location convenient as well as comfortable. Think about driving distances, perhaps using your church as a central point. Also, if childcare is offered at another location, try to limit the distance between the two locations.

You may decide to meet in several homes. In this case, be sure that someone types up a good schedule with addresses, phone numbers and clear directions to each home. Ask one woman to be in charge of this project. If there is a change in location or the schedule, it will be her responsibility to contact each woman with the change.

## CHILD CARE

If you meet during the day, you will need to decide whether or not you will provide childcare for your class. Often there is a 'golden woman' who feels called to organize the childcare and finds the helpers. Other classes leave childcare issues up to the mom. Often after the first class is finished, a friend who has had the privilege to attend is eager to help watch a friend's child so her friend can attend. She has learned the gift of serving others.

Another option is to have a childcare location and ask everyone to (donate to the pot each week) I believe each church will know the best thing to do and will make creative decisions to make it work.

Do not consider having the childcare at the same home as the class. Remember the moms need a time away. They will be distracted if their children are present, even if they are not in the room. We do allow nursing moms to bring their infants to class. This has never been a problem.

## BUDGET IDEAS

You will have to establish a budget. Will the church support this program? Do you have someone to underwrite it? The cook will need to know what amount she will have to spend in order to plan her menus (see Cooking Budget, page xx).

Let your passion for the program show when talking with your church leadership about funding. The first class is the hardest to get support for but after that, the testimony and the changed lives show the worth of the program. Feel free to use this book, *Apples of Gold*, and information from the website (**www.applesofgold.org**) as resources for sharing your vision. If the church is funding the program, they will give you an amount to spend.

Many classes look for generous donors. This might come from individuals or groups within the church, such as Sunday school classes. What a blessing these men and women are to the ministry. Be sure to keep donors informed of how the program is developing. A note now and then with a testimony will greatly encourage their hearts.

One church I know encourages women who can no longer actively participate in the ministry to sponsor an individual young woman through a class or seminar. They agree to give a specified amount. These women also make terrific prayer partners and intercessors for us. I cannot emphasize enough the need to pray for each woman who is participating.

Other programs raise money through garage and bake sales. Listen to this e-mail:

> **Betty, I just raised $980.00 in two bake sales and a garage sale. We can now start our Apples of Gold program in September. I'm so excited.**

This woman truly believed God wanted for her to start Apples of Gold in her church. She worked hard to make it happen and God honored her obedience.

## LEADERSHIP

The excitement of knowing that you have the leadership God has chosen is great motivation for the nuts and bolts of making your class happen. Each time I receive an e-mail or letter from a new class, I can literally hear the joy and excitement that is felt. I feel it too!

Assemble a list of names of women you know who love the Lord and are good potential leaders. Ask your pastor for a list of names. He may think of someone you have overlooked. Look for women who are team players. You will be working closely on this project. Be sure that there is harmony among the women involved.

Perhaps you want to start a class in your church and you are having a difficult time finding the 'golden women'. Pray! There are wonderful stories about how God called and chose women for the various Apples of Gold classes:

> **Just wanted to send you a little note of our progress. Included are the notes from our second planning meeting. Note that the mentor for the first lesson has changed. For some reason, the woman who was planning to teach this lesson felt that she should be the greeter. We then called a friend who had been wintering in Florida. She has been resting from treatments for cancer including a stem cell transplant. She was delighted to be asked and wanted to be with us all 6 weeks. The rest of us never considered calling, let alone asking her as we though she just wouldn't have the strength. She is an excellent Bible teacher and women's speaker…. Everyone is excited and ready to go.**

Every team needs a leader—someone to call meetings and keep things on target. Many times the leader is the woman who first felt the call to start Apples of Gold in her church or neighborhood. A leader can also be chosen from among the group of 'golden' women.

Gather the women who have expressed interest in participating in the Apples of Gold program as leaders. Whoever calls the meeting can function as the leader for now. The leader should have read the book *Apples of Gold* and have a good understanding of how the program works. Give general information about how this program may work in your church or neighborhood. Spend some time in prayer.

There may be issues and decisions that will take much prayer. There may be a woman who wants to mentor but who is not qualified according to scripture. It is always necessary and important to make your decisions based on scripture. Agreement among mentors is necessary on topics like Submission and Purity. Don't even attempt to start without unity among the leadership. When there is unity among the mentors, the program will go smoothly. Pray until unity is achieved.

It is important that each leader embrace the commitment being asked of her. Discuss the following Mentor's Covenant and ask each leadership woman to sign it.

## MENTOR'S COVENANT

*I covenant that I have accepted Jesus Christ as my Lord and Savior, and seek to honor Him in my life. I will seek to be a servant of the Lord in the program of Apples of Gold, having the interests of the younger women in my heart. I will prepare the lessons ahead of time, both the one I lead and the other lessons. I will faithfully pray for the Apples of Gold program and for each participant. I will, as best I can, befriend each woman in the class and make myself available to her. I will attend all six classes, the "Applesauce" meetings, and the Celebration dinner with spouses, Lord willing. If I am unable to attend a class, I will clear my absence with the other mentors.*

MENTOR'S SIGNATURE                                                      DATE ive a sign up sheet available for women who want to participate in leadership. If you have more than enough names, you may want to start more than one class. Many churches start two classes at the same time in different homes. It may be a good idea to have the names on the list reviewed by the leadership of your church. They may best know if a woman is qualified to be a leader.

## BRINGING LEADERS TOGETHER

I think it would be a good idea to ask each of the interested leaders to read the book *Apples of Gold* before the next meeting. Many churches or groups have held an Apples of Gold class for the interested mentors. They have a coffee and treat, then they do one of the lessons together, answering the questions and having discussion. Sometimes they even include a mini-version of the cooking session. This will help each leader to see what an actual class will be like and may help someone decide whether or not they are called to participate further.

I recently heard a great story about a church that was determined to start an Apples of Gold class. All the young women were lined up and eager to learn but they could not find older women to be the teaching mentors. Finally, one woman agreed to teach all the lessons. She invited several older women to attend the first class just to see what it was like. The reluctant women sat at the tables with the younger women. Listening to the sharing and observing the openness, they soon realized that indeed they could mentor. The desire to participate in the program grew and the program now has plenty of mentors.

It is important to make sure that everyone who is a mentor agrees with the program as presented. If even one mentor has a conflicting agenda, the program will be in trouble. A subject like Submission can cause differing opinions. Some women do not agree on how Submission should be taught today though I believe the Bible is quite clear about it.

The tapes of the broadcasts from Focus on the Family with Dr. Dobson and from Renewing the Heart with Janet Parshal are available from Focus. Listening to them has helped many mentors to catch the vision of Apples of Gold. You may also be able to visit another class in your area. This is the best! Seeing is believing and understanding.

I encourage the mentors in each area of the country to hold a mentor's conference once a year for the purpose of sharing ideas and encouragement. We have done this in Michigan and it is a joy to meet the wonderful mentors from the area.

We gather for a day, starting in the morning with a cup of coffee and a time for getting acquainted. Several women share and one person gives an inspirational talk. Women who teach sit with others who teach the same subject. During lunch, ideas are shared from each class. Each table has a secretary who takes notes and gives a report after lunch. These are very special days of encouragement and team building.

## STICK TO THE PLAN

The guidelines given in this book and in *Apples of Gold* come from personal experience. Since the summer of 1995, I have had a class in my home in Michigan. For several more years, I have been involved in the class in Sanibel, Florida. I have also visited several other classes as a guest. In every case, the experience is powerful and joyful.

There is only one reason I recommend that you do follow the basic outline of the program as it is clearly outlined in the book *Apples of Gold*—it works!

This by no means is intended to stifle individual creativity. It is that very creative flair that makes each lesson unique. There is plenty of room for testimonies from your life (keep it brief and to the point) that relate perfectly to the lesson you are leading. Use those stories, both funny and serious, to help the women better understand your life and character.

**It is important to think outside the lines while staying within their borders.**

As a team, agree that you will follow the program as outlined in the book. If one woman goes her own way with her lesson, teaching what she wants rather than following the book, the class is divided. It would be better if she is involved in a program where there is not a defined lesson.

This is so important because the younger women are very serious about doing their lessons at home. If they have looked up the scriptures in the lesson and answered the questions in the book, they need to have the opportunity to share those scriptures and answers in class. Otherwise, they will likely be discouraged from studying their lessons.

It is the combination of the creative talents of the mentors for each class that makes your Apples of Gold class unique. Each mentor brings her gifts to the class and shares those gifts with the class. What a blessing for the younger women to hear from many different Christian mentors how they worked through the issues of child-rearing, submission in marriage, learning how to share kindness, and hospitality.

> **I personally want to say thank you for the privilege of being a part of Apples of Gold this year. The Lord has truly given to you a vision to fill a need within the church to nurture and mentor others.**
>
> **Each week you have challenged me not only in my commitment to Christ, but to that of my husband and children. You have helped to make very clear in each week's lesson how God's Word spells out His desire for me as both a wife and mother. The mentors add so much to drive it right home when they share too!**

The letters I receive tell me that women everywhere are longing for someone to come into their lives who cares about their needs, their families, their dreams and their hurts. There is also a great need to learn how to practically take care of a home, prepare meals and share hospitality with others.

God planted a little seed that is becoming a beautiful orchard and is producing fruit that will not perish or fade away.

**Apples of Gold met my physical need for caring and pampering while deeply reaching my soul with spiritual teaching.**

## STARTING RIGHT

The decision has been made. An Apples of Gold class is starting. The 'golden women' are in place and eager to start. Enthusiasm is everywhere! What next?

It is important to have a preliminary meeting with your class. Perhaps you can invite them to a coffee or tea. At that meeting, introduce the leadership and answer any questions. Be sure that the women understand the commitment they must make to the class. In a six-week program, a class or two missed is significant.

Draw names or assign prayer partners at this meeting. This assures prayer for each woman and helps each woman connect with someone before class starts.

Ask each woman to tell a bit about her self, her family, and her personal testimony at this meeting. This will make your next meeting more comfortable and save valuable time for the lesson in your first class.

Emphasize to the classmates that they are expected to make the commitment to do their entire lesson each week. Suggest they divide the lesson up and do a portion each day and encourage them to prepare questions for you to discuss.

Ask the women to sign the Participant's Covenant. If someone indicates that she are going to miss more than one class, ask her to wait until the next time and allow another woman on the waiting list to take her place.

### PARTICIPANT'S COVENANT

*I will be a faithful participant in the Apples of gold classes, not missing more than one lesson unless it is an emergency. I will pray for the ministry of Apples of Gold, including each mentor and each classmate. I will prepare each lesson in advance, asking the Lord to give me wisdom and insight, and a heart open to obey what He shows me in the lesson and class. I desire to serve the*

*Lord and my family through the lessons learned through Apples of Gold.*

SIGNATURE                                                    DATE

At this meeting, give each young woman her folder and a copy of the book *Apples of Gold*. Each woman must have her own copy of the book and will write the answers and scriptures directly into the book. Many women refer back to their lessons and the accompanying scriptures over and over as they work through the issues studied in the lessons.

The folders can be simple and inexpensive but should be able to hold punched paper, so that each woman has a neat folder. You might ask a creative person to personalize each folder with a gold stamped apple and gold writing, or pick a folder with a slip-in sheet front. You can also print the Apples of Gold logo from the website (**www.applesof-gold.org**), add any information you like, print it in color and slip it in the front of the folders. It makes a pretty notebook.

Before your introductory meeting is over, remind the women that the discussions held in class are personal and confidential. Whatever is shared in class is to be held close to the heart. Give any last-minute instructions or directions and conclude with a time of prayer for each other and the ministry.

## A TIME AND PLACE FOR EVERYTHING

You are now ready for your first class to begin. Everything is in place. Each woman has be given some kind of folder to hold notes, recipes and other handouts from the class and has a copy of *Apples of Gold*.

You will need a GREETER for each week. Be sure the greeter is not the teaching leader for the day, but someone who is free of other duties. The greeter will meet each woman at the front door with a warm, interested greeting. She will give each woman a name tag and her recipes for the day.

It is ideal to have one mentor who is the greeter each week. A discerning greeter can tell by the step of the women coming to the door how they are doing! Here's an example in one woman's words of the impact a greeter made on her:

> **I can't tell you what a blessing you have been to me in the past several weeks at Apples of Gold. Every Tuesday as I walk up to the door and see your wonderful, smiling face, it is the perfect start to an awesome day. I loved getting to know you, learning from you, receiving your wisdom and insight and being blessed by your words. This is especially important to me because my mother is not a Christian and cannot mentor me in a biblical way.**

The greeter will look for any signs that a young woman may need special prayer or counsel. Perhaps when asked, "How are you today?" a participant may share a real need of her heart. Be sure she does not go away that day without being cared for and prayed over. Ask her to stay after class for a few minutes and have several mentors pray with her. Then assign one mentor to follow up with a phone call in a few days to see if additional help is needed.

The greeter will send everyone off to the kitchen where the cooking mentor is ready to go. Let the fun begin! Don't forget that we need to have fun together, to have a complete release from the busy-ness and tension of the day. This is the place to get acquainted with one another, to ask questions, and experiment with foods.

Most likely, someone has offered to be the cooking mentor. Every church has wonderful cooks who love to share their recipes and techniques. Perhaps you have decided to have more than one cook. The cooking section in *Apples of Gold* and this book will be just the place for them to go.

Before the lesson segment begins, ask one of the other mentors to introduce the teaching mentor for that lesson. Tell something about her family and, perhaps, a quality that makes her especially suited to facilitate this lesson. Then pray for the mentor and the hour ahead.

## QUICK TIPS FOR MENTORS
Mentors are the heart of this program. There is no limit to the impact

they can have, as evident by this participants words:

> **For me, the entire program was such a fabulous, pampering treat!**
>
> **However, I'd have to say the best part was meeting all of the mentors. To spend time with all of you who have so obviously, so lovingly, so unselfishly dedicated your lives to the Lord and to His service, was the greatest gift to me.**
>
> **Every mentor was so willing to openly share the highs and lows, the good times and struggles of living in God's Word.**
>
> **As a new Christian who struggles daily with changing my life so that I am living His word obediently, this was extremely refreshing. I now know that I am not alone in my journey. To all of you, thank you for your devotion and time to this program. Because of all of you, my faith has been strengthened immensely. May God bless all of you.**

Here are some quick tips for mentors:

- Encourage everyone, older and younger, to participate in the lesson. Sharing in the small group will likely encourage them to participate more during the tabletalk.
- Pull women into the conversation with key questions. Be patient—a few quiet moments are okay. If you're not sure you are pausing long enough, count (silently)to ten. After one woman shares, others usually follow up on their lead. One comment builds on another.
- Don't argue! Use scripture to solve issues that may come up. We can easily disagree with opinion, but it is much harder to dispute the Word of God as we read it.
- It is important to know whether each woman has made a commitment to Christ. Be sure to mention the importance of knowing Christ personally, and offer to share with anyone who has not made this commitment.

In several classes, women have accepted Christ during an Apples of Gold session. After such a joyous event, one of the mentors should offer to disciple her for several weeks in her new Christian walk. My friend, Carol Larson, who mentors both in Minneapolis and Sanibel, is very sensitive in this regard and has blessed women by giving extra time outside of class to help a woman grow in Christ.

• Be familiar with the Bible verses that speak to the issues you are teaching. Use a concordance to look up additional verses about your topic. When questions arise, answer them according to the Bible as much as you can. Avoid speculation.

• The younger women are interested in specific ways the mentors handled certain situations discussed in the lessons. Please do not just re-read the material in each paragraph, but take the highlights from each section, add your own wisdom to it, and then return to the questions in the book.

• Be sure to tell about yourself and family, but don't dominate the time. A good rule of thumb is to ask the young women to share about their families twice as often as you speak about yourself.

• Be organized. Devise a system for timing your lesson. When working on your lesson at home, time yourself. Write into the margins where you need to be at a certain time. This will help immensely in completing the main thoughts of the lesson. In one class I attend, someone discreetly holds up 15, 10, and 5 minute signs to countdown the lesson time.

• Keep on track and finish the lesson. What we are trying to do in class is cover the main thought of each section. The women will have read the lesson at home, so just read the highlights, and then add your own wisdom to that thought. Be sure to come right back to the point of the section. Stick to the lesson and complete it. I cannot emphasize this one enough. Some lessons are long, but you can divide them up so that every section of a topic is covered.

• Teach the material given. It is unfair to the women to totally make up your own lesson. The young women will be discouraged from doing the lesson in the book. They will be scrambling to try to figure out where you are and it will distract them from the important things you are trying to teach.

## WHAT ONE LESSON LOOKS LIKE

Let me give you an example of what one lesson might look like using the Kindness lesson from *Apples of Gold*. Dee, a Kindness mentor, gives each young women a copy of the book a week before class. This in itself is an act of kindness.

Begin by singing A Heart of Kindness. Printed copies of each song can be found in the back of *Apples of Gold* and may be reproduced for class use. (A sing-a-long CD is available with the songs for each lesson included. The prayer songs are sung by the worship team from my church, made up of 'polished apples'. The CD is available from the website **www.applesofgold.org**.)

Ask a couple of young women to share the answers they have written to their Apple Seeds questions, Step 1. If you do not have an immediate volunteer, ask one of the mentors to share what she has written.

Read the first paragraph (*Apples of Gold*, step 2). With that foundation, refer to the next paragraph and share from you own experience how someone has reached out to you with a similar act of kindness. Bring out a few key ideas from the paragraphs without reading it word for word. Ask the question about "what is your mental picture of a kind person?"

Next in the lesson are two passages of Scripture (*Apples of Gold*, step 2). Ask someone to read Romans 2:4 which participants should have written out in their books. It may be helpful to encourage participants who have used different Bible translations to share what they have written. Ask for volunteers to share a description of kindness.

Do the same with the next Scripture passage Psalm 103:13.

Step 3 asks questions about compassion. These types of questions are based on each participant's experiences and opinions so there are no right or wrong answers. Encourage everyone to share and honor every contribution. Next, explain the story of Elijah from 1 Kings 17:7-16.

Move on to the questions in step 4 which talk about ways God has answered prayers in your life in the past and how you are trusting Him to lead you. Check out the "Suggestions for Leaders" section at the end of the lesson for more ideas.

Next, talk about ways God has answered prayers in your life in the past and how you are trusting Him to lead you. Read 1 Thessalonians 5:15 and ask someone to share answer to question (Step 6).

Talk through paragraph about difficult relationships using personal experience or ask another mentor to share from her experience. These questions are more personal and require more self-revelation for you and the participants.

Quickly, going around the room, asking volunteers to share answers from the chart. Talk through a few of the attitudes listed that cause difficulties in relationships. Ask if anyone has a personal experience to share. Read the scriptures listed to summarize the advice given.

Pick some examples from the paragraphs in Step 7, add some of your own wisdom to these ideas and move on.

Take a good amount of time answering the questions in the "Choice Fruits" section. The lesson will be more meaningful if the participants walk away with ways to put practical kindness to work. Review the "Random Acts of Kindness". Ask for some additional ones.

"Be kind to yourself" is a very important little section. Many young women take very little time for themselves. Explain how taking time for some of their own needs gives new energy and motivation to love the others in their lives.

Encourage women to make a commitment to do one act of kindness per day for a week and then share the results in class the next week before starting the next lesson.

**WRAPPING THINGS UP**

Have a mentor or two at each table. If a buffet is used, the mentors should go through the line first, so they are seated at the table when the young women arrive. Be sure to use the Table Talk questions in *Apples of Gold* during the mealtime. If you like, make up some of your own.

How important is the time around the table? Listen to a participant tell us in her own words what this time means to her:

> **I personally want to say thank you for the privilege of being a part of Apples of Gold this year. The Lord has truly given to you a vision to fill a need within the church to nurture and mentor others.**
>
> **The cooking, lunch, and fellowship is such a 'golden' bonus. I truly feel spiritually and physically fed and emotionally strengthened in the table talk time. Each week I have found myself overwhelmed with blessings as I drive away at the end of the day. I can hardly focus on the road.**

The Table Talk questions help ensure that everyone is included in the table conversation. It is during this time that some of your most significant sharing will take place. This is a time when the practical aspects of the lesson are discussed such as "How will I show kindness to my family this week?"

Handouts are another way to keep the lesson "percolating" through the week. These can range from small notes with a key verse to reading lists to practical household tips. Here are a few examples:

### What a Sheet of Bounce Can Do
1) Repel mosquitoes. Tie a sheet through a belt loop when outdoors.
2) Eliminate static electricity from TV screen/computer monitor by rubbing with a used sheet.
3) Dissolve soap scum from shower doors.
4) Freshen the air in a closet or drawer
5) Prevent thread from tangling (run a threaded needle to eliminate static cling)
6) Prevent static cling by rubbing a damp, used sheet over panty hose
7) Place a sheet in luggage before storing.
8) Put a sheet under the front seat to freshen the air in the car.

9) Place a sheet in your coat pocket to avoid shock getting out of the car in winter.
10) Remove baked-on food from a cooking pan. Put sheet in pan, fill with water, soak overnight, sponge clean.
11) Place a sheet in the bottom of wastebaskets to eliminate odors.
12) Collect cat hair by rubbing the area with a sheet.
13) Wipe window blinds with a sheet to prevent dust from resetting
14) Wipe (up) sawdust from drilling or sandpaper. Works like a tack cloth. eliminate odors in dirty laundry.
15) Deodorize shoes or sneakers by placing a sheet in them overnight. (Baking soda sprinkled in sneakers does this also.)

## HOUSEHOLD HINTS

1) To eliminate onion, garlic or bleach odor from your hands, dampen your hands and rub them on a stainless steel sink.
2) To remove stains from a tablecloth, soak the item in denture tablets.
3) To clean up a broken egg on the floor, sprinkle salt, allow to stand a few minutes, then sweep it up.
4) To open a sealed envelope, place in the freezer for a few hours, then slide a knife under the flap.

## FOOD RESCUES

1) Hard Brown Sugar – Put a slice of fresh bread in the bag or container.
2) Over-salted Vegetables – Pour boiling water over them, drain and taste, or put a raw potato in the pot for a few minutes.
3) Soggy Mashed Potatoes – add a few spoonfuls of instant mashed potatoes.
4) Cooked Tomato Dish – Add a small amount of sugar to enhance the tomato flavor.
5) Scorched Food in the Pan – Remove to another pan. DO NOT SCRAPE THE STUCK PAN. Place baking soda in the scorched pan plus water and reheat to remove the stuck items.

## MEMENTOS AND REMINDERS

It is certainly not necessary to give a favor each week, but it is a nice reminder of the lesson. A bookmark with a verse from the lesson made on the computer, laminated and punched with a pretty ribbon tied through the top is a nice memento.

Here are some additional ideas for each lesson from one Apples of Gold class:

- Lesson 1—for a daily reminder of the Proverbs 25:11 passage, we bought magnetic 3 x 5 inch refrigerator picture sleeves, printed out the verse from the computer on some very pretty paper, and cut it to size. Then we put silver rickrack around the edges of the frame and added a pretty silver bow with a gold-painted wooden apple glued in the center to corner of each frame.

- Lesson 2—a little white votive candle placed in a pretty silver pot with a bit of decoration added.

- Lesson 3—a tiny pot with live miniature violets.

- Lesson 4—a tiny goblet with flowers hot-glued to the stem of the glass. The glass looks like a tiny tulip.

- Lesson 5— little heart box painted cream with maroon accents, tiny bow and flowers in the middle of the lid.

- Lesson 6—a napkin basket with a package of napkins.

One mentor made a little packet of homemade seasoning, put it in a little jar tied with a ribbon. The attached note talked about how our lives must be seasoned and tenderized with the Word of God.

Mary gives each woman a small plastic photo album to carry in her purse. She talks about how special it makes a child feel that mom carries photos of him or her everywhere she goes. She lets the women know that she might check up on them. At the celebration dinner, Mary goes from table to table looking at the albums.

You could also give a small package of thank you notes and a reminder that it is important to send notes of appreciation to those who have ministered to you. Or, fill a Mug of Love with tea bags or cocoa, tie with a pretty ribbon, and give as an encouragement to be kind to yourself.

Remember, it's not the size or cost of the gift that matters. Giving as a demonstration of love and hospitality is what counts. It is your personal creativity that makes each class unique and special.

CHAPTER 4

The Cooking Mentor

## THE IMPORTANCE OF HOSPITALITY

I am often asked why food and cooking are a part of Apples of Gold. When God called me to start this ministry, it is the idea that God clearly gave me. There needs to be a balance between the practical and spiritual, but both are needed to encourage women today. Our homes need to be a haven for our families, the place they long to be at the end of the day, and a place of joy and peace. One of the ways to start is by encouraging and nurturing women, teaching ways to make home that special place.

Where there's a will, there's a way, truly applies to this cooking section. Please do not even consider eliminating this much-needed hour in the kitchen. Our families need help in this area. Christian families must find ways to sit at dinner together.

It is certainly more important that we teach spiritual lessons to the women than that we cook together. But as I study the Word of God there are many examples of how food and fellowship are part of that learning process.

> *Offer hospitality to one another without grumbling. Each one should use whatever gift he has received to serve others, faithfully administering God's grace in its various forms. 1 Peter 4:9*

As Jesus traveled from village to village, He was often ministered to by friends and strangers who welcomed Him into their homes, took care of His needs, and fed Him.

Mary, Martha, and Lazarus, Nicodemus, Matthew, and many more ministered to Christ with their hospitality.

In His last hours on earth, with the shadow of the cross hanging over Him, Jesus shared the Last Supper with His disciples. Jesus had important things to say to the disciples that night. He chose to share those things around the table. Jesus also commanded that His sacrifice be remembered by the church with the breaking of bread.

For the early church, hospitality was part of their witness to those who didn't know Jesus as Lord. "They broke bread in their homes and ate together with glad and sincere hearts, praising God and enjoying the favor of all the people" Acts 2:46.

After Jesus had spoken to the multitudes and healed many of the sick, He recognized their need for physical food and had compassion on them. The disciples balked and Jesus persisted while the disciples fretted over the cost of such hospitality. Everyone was satisfied with 12 baskets left over. This story is a fine example of hospitality. Though I truly love a party, I hope never to have the challenge of feeding 5,000.

Sometimes we, like the disciples, worry about the expense and inconvenience of hospitality. There is a monetary cost when we prepare a meal for someone. Sometimes it may even be a sacrifice to serve others with your hospitality, but the Lord will provide the blessing when we follow His example.

What is it about food that is so sociable? We love to meet at the local coffee or bagel shop to chat with a friend. We gather on a hot evening at the ice cream shop for a cone, or in our town, for a "Tommy Turtle," a hot fudge and caramel sundae with salted nuts, whipped cream and a cherry!

Many of us are looking for new ways to delight our family and friends at the table. The three "P's"— planning, purchasing and preparing—are a 'very daily', often monotonous fact of life. It is good to have a new slant on cooking, some shortcuts, planning and organizing help, and ideas for leftovers.

Has anyone ever visited you and stayed longer than you expected? We have experienced such guests on a few occasions. It is getting close to lunch or dinner and you begin to wonder what is hiding in your refrigerator or pantry that is fit to serve. It always amazes me that somehow there is something to eat, that our guests are grateful and complimentary, and that there is usually food left over.

Some of the best times of spiritual blessing in our home have been tied to sharing our dinner table with friends—old and new, or strangers we have just met on their way to becoming friends. I am so convinced "There is no place like home" for sharing food and the "good news of Christ" hand in hand.

Friendships for a lifetime have been made in our home. Joyous occasions such as bridal showers, engagement parties, Christmas open house, dinner with a new family from church, and especially having our children and grandchildren at home are some of those good times. Other times tears are spilled as trials come and friends need a safe harbor in which to share a confidence or we need to share our struggles and sorrows together.

It's a blessing to minister to a weary friend, telling her to put her feet up while you prepare a hot cup of tea for her. At times, I have tucked a pillow under a friend's head and covered her with a quilt. Many times, friends have ministered to me in similar ways. Blessings await us when we willing reach out to others. Take it from Cosa—here is her story:

> **Dear Betty,**
> **My husband and I just returned from visiting our daughter and her family in Washington D.C. I can't tell you how special and loved we both felt the entire time we were there. Our daughter had a beautiful bouquet of daffodils by our bed with a basket of brochures, maps, etc. My favorite soap and bubble bath were placed in our bathroom, and our favorite coffee was brought to us each morning with breakfast in bed on Saturday.**
> **The frosting on the cake was when our daughter drew**

**a fabulous bubble bath in their Jacuzzi tub with candles glowing all around.**

**We have never been pampered like this. Our daughter said it was all because of her experience in Apples of Gold. WOW...thank you!**

It is a joy to teach these principles to the young women in Apples of Gold—home skills such as cooking, obedience to the Word of God, and hospitality to family and friends—all as part of the joy of being a servant to others. Who knows! in so doing they may be entertaining "angels unaware" (Hebrews 13:1-2).

## AN HEIRLOOM OPPORTUNITY

In days past, moms and daughters worked hand in hand in the kitchen, and young women left the home with a good knowledge of food and its preparation. They also had the blessing of working with mom, even if they may not have realized how much that relationship would affect their life.

I believe there is in this day a growing desire to revisit that era. There is a growing interest in cooking and baking. The Food Channel is popular and is expanding to include many different food experiences. On these programs, the knowledge and preparation of food is made fun and exciting. We are being educated how to prepare a well-balanced menu, how to make food both delicious and lovely to look at, we are learning how important cleanliness is in preparing food, and we are being taught that we can do it!

The Food Channel is fun to watch, I enjoy it. I recommend that the cooking mentor take some time to watch. We can learn much about techniques, how to choose certain foods, variations in cooking styles, and how to demonstrate recipes to the class.

But watching the cooking channel does not allow me to have a personal relationship with those teaching me.

Working side by side in the kitchen at home provides an intergenerational opportunity for nurturing as well as teaching. My friend Nancy, a 'super grandma' and mentor, includes her grandchildren in meal planning, preparation, and presentation of the table. What a wonderful way to have one-on-one time with a grandchild. They may just come to grandma with a heart need one day because of the special relationship that has been established in the kitchen.

One mentor told me that she regrets never allowing her daughters in the kitchen when they were young. As a result, they cannot cook. But it's never too late. Now her daughters are in Apples of Gold.

I am so thankful that our daughters are good cooks. It is such a joy to eat a meal that they have prepared just for us. If we teach the basics at home, our daughters will have the confidence to try new things in their own homes. Now, I sometimes ask them for recipes!

The opportunity to work together in the kitchen with my children and grandchildren is one I cherish. It is worth the first few messes to see a child succeed in making those first chocolate chip cookies, or teaching how to roll a pie crust and later share the finished product together. You will find the kids peeking into the oven to see how 'their' pie is doing.

I am thankful that our children are teaching our grandchildren how to cook. A couple of the boys enjoy grilling. Our eleven-year-old grandson, Marcus, was involved in a class project raising money for the homeless. He wanted to give more than he had on hand to give. He decided to make fudge and sell it in his neighborhood. After selling the first batch in short order, he made a second batch and did the same. He made fifty dollars for his school project and learned a wonderful lesson about the joy of serving others. He also gave me a hint about improving the taste of my fudge recipe by using a different kind of chocolate!

Our granddaughter, Carly, loves to cook. At eleven, she sometimes makes the entire meal for her family. Her mom has allowed her to mess up the kitchen a bit in order to learn. I remember baking together when she had to stand on a stool to reach the counter. Her tiny fingers could make prettier pastry tarts than my large finger could make. We made candy for the Christmas Bazaar at school and wrapped it in pretty bags. She was so exited when every bag sold!

Recently, Carly and her friend prepared a complete dinner for their parents. They set the table with the best china, walked through the fields and collected wild flowers for the centerpiece, cooked the dinner, put on their best dresses and served the meal. They had such a great time. How excited she was to send photos of the event to me.

Preparing a lovely meal for our family provides not only physical nutrition, but food for the soul as well. When we sit at the dinner table as a family, our children have our undivided attention. It can be a time of lively discussion and a great teaching time as well.

First Corinthians 6:19 states that our body is a temple of the Holy Spirit. We need to care for it and nourish it. A new baby is given the best possible nourishment. As our children grow, they have the same need for good, healthy food. Without proper care, they will not grow to their best potential.

Giving our family the best possible foods is our responsibility. Providing good nutrition for our family is an act of service, a high calling. When we serve joyfully, we are teaching our children to do the same.

We can teach them how to plan, shop for and create delicious and nutritious meals for their families and also make it an enjoyable experience. Many women have not had the experience of learning from their moms when they were young. Now they have a family to feed and they need help and encouragement.

Perhaps they lack confidence as well as know-how, having never hosted a dinner party, brunch, or shower. Cooking class just may be the confidence booster they need. Listen to the note of accomplishment and confidence in this testimonial:

> **What a blessing the Apples of Gold program has been in our lives!**
>
> **Thank you. It seems that I am always sharing about the program with someone! I feel privileged to have been a part of it. The lessons take on new meaning everyday and God speaks to me more and more.**
>
> **I am now a celebrated cook! What fun I am having sharing the gift of hospitality. I will pray for this program.**

## TEACHABLE MOMENTS

If your children are hanging around the kitchen, they may not only be hungry for food, they may be hungry for your time and attention. Sometimes they simply want to be near you. These are teachable moments. Let them help, give them a task, and take the time to teach it correctly. Each task learned eases your kitchen burden. Or, let them learn from watching you. Prop them up on a stool and have a good conversation.

Perhaps while you are occupied with preparing dinner, your child may feel comfortable enough to share a deep need with you. I truly believe the kitchen is that comfortable spot in the home where the more casual atmosphere encourages spontaneous sharing. Invite your family back into the kitchen and watch as you begin to connect in ways you may never have connected before.

Teaching how to clean up the kitchen is part of the learning process. It is not only easier to work in a clean kitchen, it is an important health issue. Teach your children about using clean dishcloths and towels, about wiping the counters with hot, soapy water, and to clean the chopping block after cutting raw meat and before cutting up the fruit for dessert. As you are working together, opportunities for teaching will pop up. Use them!

### TEAMWORK

In the kitchen all alone—chopping, blending, baking;
Feeling sorry for myself while others time are taking
   for reading, laughing, having fun;
How exhausting it can be.

In the kitchen, all of us—chopping, blending, baking;
Oh, how quickly time now flies, special time we're making
   for sharing, laughing, having fun;
Soon our work will all be done! How rewarding that will be.

No longer sighs of "me, me, me" but joyful sounds of "we, we, we".
What a different kind of tone than in the kitchen all alone.

Wouldn't it be wonderful to have a return to the dinner table in our homes? So many families are missing the enjoyment of being together around the dinner table. We are missing the opportunity of good conversation, and sharing good food with our family. We are missing the opportunity to pray together and have devotions at the table. We are missing the laughter of a child's best joke of the day.

Sometimes dinner is the joke! Our grandson, Nick was complimenting our daughter, Lisa on the delicious dinner she had prepared. Lisa replied, "Thanks, Nick! Mom cooked gourmet tonight." Nicolas responded, "Wow, it tastes just like chicken."

## WELCOME TO APPLES OF GOLD

With this background about the importance of hospitality and why Apples of Gold is helpful to young wives and moms, let's examine what a typical class might look like.

After being greeted warmly at the door by a mentor, the women are given a nametag and the recipes for the day. On the first day, each woman is given a folder or notebook. The folder has been decorated with a gold apple and marked Apples of Gold. Be creative! Perhaps someone in your group is an artist, or is involved with "stamping". The recipes are printed on standard size paper and punched. The young women are making a recipe book a week at a time. They will write all their notes on the pages, so they can prepare the recipes easily at home.

Our greeter then urges them on to the kitchen for a timely start. A small, delectable treat awaits them. The treat can be a wonderful 'smoothie' to drink made with fresh fruits, or a 'garden vegetable' drink. This would be served in just a sampling size cup. It could be a cracker with a wonderful dip, perhaps displayed in a halved red pepper. It may be a cookie or a mini-muffin. Mostly, it is simply a "welcome to the kitchen" treat.

This treat is a good conversation starter. "Oh, isn't this yummy?" "Did you ever taste anything like this before?" " I hope I can prepare this at home. My family would love this!" Swap kitchen anecdotes like the following:

**One evening after dinner at our home, our grandson, Lee, said, "Nan, this food was YUMMYLICIOUS!**

Serving the treat in the kitchen helps the women to gather where the class begins. If food is served in the living room or dining room, it will be harder to bring everyone back to the kitchen. It also takes away from class time. Beside that, we all know that everyone enjoys hanging around the kitchen!

It is the cook's responsibility to start class on time. If the cooking starts late, the lesson starts late. This is unfair to the person facilitating the next portion of the class.

## THE JOY OF COOKING

The cooking mentor should cook with as much joy as skill. That enjoyment of cooking will spill over from her heart to the heart of the women. Cooking class needs to be light-hearted and fun as well as helpful. It is a release from the cares of the day.

In class, we learn about basic cooking and not-so-basic cooking. We want to go beyond Mac-and-Cheese 101, but also want to prepare foods that are not intimidating to the women. This is a "you can do it" hour.

I often share about my 'cooking flops and failures' like the rhubarb custard pies I made for a dinner party. I had worked very hard on the lattice tops. The pies were so pretty. When dessert time came, I served each guest a slice of the pie with a scoop of ice cream and waited for the compliments. My guests were politely eating the pie when my husband said, "Honey, have you tasted this pie?" I took a bite and realized I had forgotten the sugar. Talk about pucker power! All I could do was laugh. The guests ate their ice cream.

Another time in class, I opened the refrigerator to fetch the box of blueberries for the top of our dessert. They were in a plastic box with a lid attached. When I reached for the box, the lid flew open and blueberries scattered across the kitchen floor. In my haste to try to rescue the blueberries, I knocked over a jar of simple syrup (water and sugar mixture). It joined the blueberries on the floor. Needless to say, it brought the class to a complete halt as everyone scrambled to help with cleanup. It also brought gales of laughter. What else could we do?

The way the cook reacts to burned biscuits and other disasters will determine how the young women will react when it happens to them…and it will, sooner or later. Above all, keep your sense of humor.

**It is said that most accidents happen in the kitchen—
and most families eat them.**

If you are relaxed about the cooking, you can share some of your cooking stories with the women as you are mixing or kneading. Use these times to allow for questions or stories from the women as well. It helps us to get to know one another better.

When I visited a class in Minneapolis a few years ago, the cook for the day was Evie Young. She was then 85 years old. She kneaded her bread with vigor and joy. She prepared a complete Swedish meal for the women. She was an inspiration to everyone.

I recently received evaluations from the Minneapolis class of 2001. One young woman commented about how Evie touched her heart. She is still sharing at the age of 88 her wonderful knowledge of baking and cooking with the younger women.

A good cook clearly describes each recipe as she prepares it. It is important to assume nothing. Even such things as loosely packed or tightly packed cups of brown sugar need to be explained. Questions like "Should I use butter or margarine?" "What kind of oil is best to use?" and "What does it mean to julienne vegetables?" are bound to come up.

**One cook told the women to grease the bottom of the pan.
One woman did just that. She greased the very OUTSIDE
bottom of the pan!**

A good cook also asks for questions, listens carefully, and tries to answer each question. If she does not have the answer to the question, she asks another mentor, or one of the young women if they know the answer. Engaging the entire class is so important. Have the women gather closely around so they can truly see what you are doing.

Because this is such a happy, chatty time, you may have to stop and ask for the attention of the women. That is okay! If you sense a woman is really struggling with a cooking skill, suggest quietly that you will help her later, one on one, so that she will not be embarrassed in front of the entire class.

It is a good idea to ask certain questions the first week such as:

- Does anyone have a food allergy?
- Is there something the class especially wants to learn?
- What are family favorite foods that we can dress up a bit?

It is also interesting and helpful to planning to have a theme: Italian, Greek, Chinese, Picnic, Baby Shower, etc. But make certain that at least some of the foods on the menu will appeal to each member of the family. For example, in our Chinese food class we prepare Sweet and Sour Chicken along with more exotic Beef with Oyster Sauce.

On the day "Loving Your Children" is taught, it is fun to prepare foods especially for children that day. Pasta dishes, cookies, breads, variety pizzas and smoothie drinks are favorites. I have made crown cakes for little princesses, pickle frogs for the prince, a pooch from a hoagie bun with donut hole cheeks, a carrot tail, and hot dog legs. Look in magazines for ideas. I once sent the crown cake home with a mom whose child had a birthday that day.

If several cooks are used in your class, I suggest that you plan all the menus before you start your program. That will eliminate misunderstandings among the cooks and allow them to plan their menu knowing it will not be repeated. We may not want six weeks of chicken. It is important to teach the preparation of a variety of meats. If possible, prepare nutritious dishes not common such as fish and perhaps a vegetarian meal.

I typically demonstrate five or six recipes in class. Some recipes are given that are not demonstrated in class, such as a cookie or brownie recipe with a unique taste. Most women know how to make those items, but welcome having some new recipes.

If the women are expecting lunch, be sure your menu is complete. Soup, salad, and dessert or a salad with meat, bread and dessert. Desserts are always a big hit!

## RESPONSIBILITY OF COOKING MENTOR

The cooking mentor has many and varied responsibilities. One of the most important skills she will need is good organization. It is also important that she teaches organizational skills to the women. Planning ahead is vital for a successful class. It is also important to have helpers on the day of class, to prep foods, finish a task and keep ahead of the cleanup. The helpers are volunteer "Polished Apples" from previous classes. They love to return to stay connected.

It is helpful if another mentor, not the cook, is assigned the responsibility of lining up helpers. My friend, Linda Topp, types up the list of helpers with the date they will be working and also gives a copy to me. If a helper needs to cancel, she is responsible for calling Linda, who finds a substitute. She also calls to confirm the schedule with the volunteer. This saves the cooking mentor so much time and she can be sure she will have the help she needs.

## PLANNING THE MENU

When planning your menu, look at the overall picture first. Before choosing the recipes, consider the number of people you will be serving and how that will affect your budget and the amount of food you must prepare.

**Fancy or Frugal**—Looking at how much you have to spend on this particular dinner or lunch may also influence what you prepare and how you will prepare it. Is this a fancy dinner where you are will ing to splurge a bit, or is this more of a casserole, salad, and bread kind of meal?

**Who's Coming to Dinner**—What does the guest list look like? Will you be serving adults, women only, or are there children and teens included in this party? You will want to serve food appropriate for all who are attending and food they will love to eat.

**Be realistic!**—Don't get caught short by choosing a menu that is too difficult or time consuming. Be sure you have refrigerator space available for the amount of food you purchase. If you are overwhelmed, your guests will feel it. For a large crowd, prepare something familiar that you know tastes wonderful and that turns out every time.

**Plan Ahead**—Try to plan make-ahead items into your menu so you can concentrate on your guests. Plan your table service ahead. Do you have enough dishes, silverware, and serving utensils for this meal? How about ice, napkins, serving platters? Lay everything out a couple days before to be sure you have not forgotten anything essential.

**Consider the Season**—A hot summer evening is not the best time for a bowl of chili, but a beautiful salad with meat is refreshing. Try to use fruits and vegetables that are in season. They will be fresher and may cost less as well. Is there anything as wonderful as the first strawberry shortcake in June or a bowl of Autumn soup full of root vegetables in October? Be creative and use foods in new and varied ways. Try Pumpkin Soup or Cold Raspberry Soup. You and your guests will enjoy trying new foods.

**Be Thematic**—Keep your menu in balance. If you are serving Wet Burritos, be sure that your salad has a strong flavor as well, and that appetizers are Tex-Mex. Try to decorate for the theme. I find many wonderful ideas by paging through books and magazines. Adapt ideas to fit your budget and table. Your party will seem planned from the first impression of the table to the food and fun. And your friends will appreciate your efforts to do something special for them.

One of the greatest helps to me in planning the menu is having all my recipes on the computer. There are several different types of software available. I use Master Cook. It is simple to use. The program comes with other cookbooks already installed and you can set a separate, named file for your own recipes. Having your own named file allows you to see only the recipes you want for your class.

Computer programs can often be found on sale. I found some on sale for $12 and gave one to each daughter for Christmas. Then I gave them my files so they can make a cookbook of their own to pass on to their children and friends.

Entering the recipes may seem like a big job at first, but it is well worth the effort. To begin, enter only the recipes you plan to use in class. This is such a time-saver in the long run. With a touch of the button, your recipes are printed for each woman.

If you are a mentor who does not use the computer, it should be easy to find a volunteer to type them for you. It is important that each woman has easy to read recipes. Having them on the computer assures that each time a recipe is copied, it will be in the same format. All the recipes for the day must be printed, punched, and collated before class. This is a great job to hand off to a helper or a husband since as cook you will be very busy preparing for your class.

I now have over 600 of my well-loved recipes on my computer. I have recipes from my grandmother, mother, aunts and friends, even from my daughters. By entering a few every time I was working on the computer, the project was completed. If a friend asks for a recipe, I can print it quickly and she is saved the time of writing it down. It also prevents mistakes made in hand-copying. No longer do I have to search all my little scraps of paper, and notes for a certain recipe. They are all filed by category and easy to find. And menu planning is a snap!

## CHOOSING THE RECIPES

There are many things to consider when planning the menu such as taste, color, texture, and variety. Most good cooks already know these things, but I find it helpful to look through magazines for attractive ways to prepare food.

If you are a cooking mentor, you most likely have some good cookbooks. Browsing cookbooks is a good way to help you plan your menu for each week. Some cookbooks are even designed by menu and would be helpful in choosing well-balanced menus.

Many of the younger women may not have been taught about food presentation. Show the women how you would display each menu on a plate, reminding them that white chicken looks more appetizing when served with green beans and red tomatoes. Pasta and red sauce look beautiful with a mixed green salad and white bread. Having a pretty dinner is nearly important as having a delicious one. It may even encourage a child who is not an especially adventuresome eater. Just a simple garnish or parsley can dress up a plate.

The following are some suggestions for menus from some of our wonderful Apples of Gold cooks:

- A tailgate picnic
- Uses for frozen breads and other frozen foods
- A salad trio consisting of Seafood Salad, Chicken Salad, Greek Salad served with dessert
- Mexican Food
- Leftovers eaten by candlelight. Pull leftovers from your refrigerator, be creative, and start a new tradition
- Chicken, Chicken, Chicken. Three ways to make chicken (soup, salad, and casserole) can be used to demonstrate how to cook chicken while making stock, and how to use rotisserie chicken from the deli on a busy day.
- Cookie making—great for Christmas
- Chinese menu
- Brunch menu
- Soup, Salad, Bread
- A formal tea with sandwiches and cakes
- Dessert only! If you have a dessert only class, be sure to inform the class the week before so they can eat something nutritious before they arrive.
- Sauces—how to a make basic white sauce, stock, gravy, béarnaise, homemade mayonnaise, barbeque sauce, etc.

## TECHNIQUES TO DEMONSTRATE

If there is a technique you want to demonstrate, have the necessary equipment ready. When demonstrating how to chop onions, you may include the methods of sharpening knives, and suggest what kind of knives are helpful to own.

In our Sanibel, FL class, Nancy's husband, John comes in to teach the women how to sharpen knives. It is such a wonderful idea and a testimony of teamwork in that home. He even made a clever wooden box that keeps the knife at the correct angle while sharpening.

If you are teaching the art of making pastry, you may want to demonstrate the hand method and the method of using a food processor. Many women do not have a food processor, though I think it is a great gift. I use mine so very often, but it is important to teach how to make do with what you have and even how to be creative when you don't have the specified kitchen utensil or equipment.

Teaching how to sauté foods can be difficult if the women cannot easily see the stove. Try using an electric skillet placed directly on the counter in front of them.

When doubles are needed, prepare one ahead and freeze. For instance, if you are serving cake, you will need to have one completed because there is not enough time to bake, cool and frost a cake in class. It is still important to demonstrate the preparation of the cake in class. A frozen dessert is another example of a make-ahead necessity.

It would be impossible to prepare a beef roast dinner in class and have it done in one hour. In that case, I save a small amount of the roast, or prepare a second small one in class for our family dinner or to bring to a friend who would appreciate having a surprise dinner delivered to her door.

You may be surprised to know that many of the young women have never prepared a pot roast dinner. Some families may even think they do not like pot roast because they have never had a deliciously browned and seasoned roast served to them with the meat literally falling off the bone.

There are so many foods that can be prepared from the leftovers of a large beef or pork roast and from chicken. These leftover dishes can save hours of meal preparation. Learning how to properly freeze left-overs is essential. It is important to also teach how to store foods in the refrigerator because foods can spoil quickly if not properly stored.

Try to have some "hands on" demonstrations even if only a few women can participate. It is a confidence builder for the women to see that they can do as you do. I often pass a small piece of pastry or dough around, so the women can feel the texture of the food. It helps them when they prepare it at home to know what bread dough should feel like as well as how it looks.

> **Susan teaches cooking in a class in Grand Rapids, Michigan. In one class, she demonstrated bread making. In order to be very thorough, she had batches of dough ready in varying stages including baking. On the following week of class, she opened one of her ovens to Bake something in class. Behold, a loaf of bread from last week. She demonstrated it as a doorstop! I believe that is called thinking on your feet.**

Teach how to beat egg whites for meringues and how not to make it on a humid day. Teach how to fold egg whites into a cake. Some young women have never been shown how to separate an egg. Don't assume that the women know how to do this or any other skill properly.

Prepare an herb chart, showing the women how to use herbs in their recipes and perhaps how to grow them as well. This would be a great hand-out to duplicate for each woman's notebook.

Teach also how to store herbs. Fresh herbs are more fragile than dried herbs but are also more flavorful. Because they are more perishable, pur-chase in amounts you will use fairly soon. Herbs can be kept fresh in the refrigerator short-term by placing stems in a glass with a small amount of water. Dried herbs should be labeled and kept in a cool spot in the kitchen (not too near the stove). Remind the women that dried herbs are generally good for only about one year.

Most recipes are written for dried herbs. If using fresh herbs, you may need to increase the amount up to three times what the recipe indicates. My favorite cookbook about herbs is The Best of Thymes by Margie Clark. Each chapter describes a different herb and the recipes include in each chapter reflect that herb.

Another favorite of mine is Christmas Thyme at Oak Hill Farm. It is such a beautiful book full of ideas for Christmas parties, decorations, and recipes. My copy was autographed by the author, Margie Clark, before she was killed tragically in an automobile accident near her farm home in Indiana a few years ago. If you have difficulty finding it in the bookstores, contact the publisher at Thyme Cookbooks, Marge Clark, Oak Hill Farm, 6242 West State Road 28, West Lebanon, IN 47991-8054.

Teach how to properly grease and flour a pan, how to use parchment paper or the wonderful product "Silpat". Silpat is a Teflon product that comes made to size or ready to cut. Placed on a cookie sheet, there is no need for greasing the pan ever. Just wipe or rinse after use and it is ready for another use.

Show the art of melting chocolate and describe the benefits of simple syrup. Demonstrate how to whip cream without turning it to butter. Make different marinades and rubs and use them in grilling. The list of skills to demonstrate can go on and on.

Having all the foods for a meal ready at the proper time seems to be a challenge for some women. Teach how to remedy that problem by teaching organizational skills.

Most of all, be sure the women know that experience has been your teacher, that you have had your share of 'flops' and that you are there to help in anyway you can. I receive calls from women who need a quick answer about a certain recipe or how to remedy a problem. I enjoy that special contact with the women.

**My friend Sue was making a chocolate "Wacky Cake".**

**Perhaps you are familiar with the recipe. The dry ingredients are placed directly into the pan. A hole is made in the middle and the liquid ingredients are added. The pan had been in the oven for several minutes one of the young women noticed the eggs still on the counter. Sue acted surprised and said, "Oh, dear, what shall we do?"**

**The women responded, "Can you still add them in?"**

**Sue removed the cake from the oven, added the eggs, stirred them in and returned the cake to the oven.**

**It turned out fine.**

**Though Sue made "lemonade from lemons" that day, that trick may not always work!**

## THE DAY OF CLASS

Reminder: Start on time. Have a treat ready! Have helpers lined up for the day. The first time you have a class you may ask some friends to help you with cooking and cleanup. It is so beneficial to have extra hands in the kitchen.

After the first class, you will ask 'Applesauce" women to help. There are many of these "polished apples"—women who have participated in Apples of Gold previously and willingly come back to serve and to experience class again.

Some foods are partially demonstrated by the cook and then passed on to the helpers for completion. For example, mix the ingredients for meatballs, demonstrate how to make nice round meatballs with an ice cream or melon scoop, talk about how to cook or bake, then pass the remaining meat mixture to the helpers. They can complete the task, and I can move to another recipe.

If I make Risotto, or another food that needs constant watching or stirring on the stove, the helpers stir the pot. They wash pans that may need to be re-used like the bowl of the electric mixer or a sauté pan.

When the cooking hour is complete, we all leave the kitchen for the next hour while the helpers finish preparing all the food. They understand that it must be ready in one hour for lunch. If the food is not ready, the Table Talk time is shortened.

I ask the helpers to come a bit early to give instructions for the morning. I often write a sheet of instructions for them. It is important that they understand clearly what you expect from them, and how to make it happen. That understanding keeps them from being frazzled or unsure of themselves in front of the others.

I try to have the serving dishes and utensils ready, drinks ready to serve, giving instructions to the helpers on things like whether food will be buffet style or served at the table.

I enjoy the support the helpers give in showing that they have learned how to be confident and competent in the kitchen, a great encouragement to a fledgling cook. And mostly, I love the opportunity to once again share a lovely morning with them. These are truly women I love and cherish.

After class, these precious friends will help clean up the dishes and make the kitchen shine. After seven years, they know my kitchen pretty well and can even place cleaned dishes and pots back in their proper place. The cook truly appreciates the helpers!

## KITCHEN CLEANLINESS

Wash your hands after each procedure with soap and warm water. Dry with a clean cloth. Talk about cross-contamination of foods from improper handling. Being conscientious about working in a clean and safe manner is an important lesson to demonstrate to your students and will make them feel more comfortable eating food from your kitchen.

Have several clean dishcloths and towels ready for use in class. If you are wiping up after cutting or working with raw chicken, teach the women to rinse the cloth and then put it in the laundry. Do not use that same cloth for the rest of the class. Statistics also show that sponges and dishcloths carry many germs.

It is good to talk about general kitchen cleanliness including the stove, the refrigerator, and the sink. Teaching how cleaning as we cook not only helps to keep the kitchen clean but it can keep us from being frustrated. It is far easier to clean a stove immediately than to remove baked-on dirt. Teach the importance of cleaning the chopping surfaces, using bleach after cutting chicken to destroy germs. I keep bleach under my sink just for that purpose.

I like to teach that coming into a clean kitchen in the morning is well worth the effort of doing all the dishes from dinner. It gives your day a brighter start. It can be quite discouraging to walk into a kitchen full of dirty dishes in the morning when you are busy organizing your day.

## SUGGESTING COOKBOOKS AND RECIPES

It is a nice idea to suggest just a few cookbooks that are helpful to you and one that teaches the basic cooking skills. Some cookbooks have ideas for menu planning, decorating and setting the table, proper etiquette, food terms, and techniques. Choose your favorites because you will have better knowledge of those books and you can tell why you like them.

Ask the other women if they have a favorite recipe or cookbook. It is a good conversational tool. It might be fun to have a recipe exchange one week with each woman bringing copies of her favorite family recipe for the entire class.

## THE FINER THINGS

Many women have grown up without being taught how to set a table or proper etiquette at the table. It is a good idea to explain why you have set the tables a certain way. For instance, if you are serving soup and have added a soupspoon, explain where it is positioned at the table.

I like to prepare a place setting on my kitchen island at times to demonstrate the setting for the day. On a pretty place mat, I place all the china, glassware, utensils, and napkin.

A few words of simple explanation on which fork to use or what to do with a napkin can save a person from embarrassment at the table.

One of the mentors, Sandy, has a drawing of a correct place setting sketched on the recipes for the day. That is also a very helpful idea. This is one of those "don't assume anything" categories.

You can help the women to understand that it is a blessing to their family to be called to a pretty table, even on Monday night. It doesn't take any longer to set the table correctly. If you teach the children, they can take turns helping you.

> *Mom taught me well to set the table—fork on left, knife on right.*
> *And as a child we kept the rule "Candles just at night."*
> *But now that I am grown up, I let my family know*
> *Just how special they are to me with "daylight" candle glow.*

## FAMILY OR GUESTS

We need to treat of family like guests and our guests like family. One of the participants listened the first week as I shared how important it is to set a pretty table for our family. The next week she shared that in nine years of marriage, she did not have matching silverware and used whatever she had. After listening in class, she decided to purchase a complete set. She shared that every single person in the family commented on how nice the table looked and how they appreciated that one small act!

Don't forget to use napkins! Paper napkins are fine for everyday, but it is nice to have some good cloth napkins as well. Sometimes we demonstrate napkin folding. Look for napkins on sale. Sometimes they are a dollar or less in a discount store. Don't save them just for company—use them often. Your family will notice and appreciate them.

It is also a good idea to share the importance of thank you notes and of responding to invitations. If the invitation says RSVP, the hostess is counting on the person to send a response. How frustrating it is to have to call everyone to know whether or not they will be attending after sending a written invitation. Teach that it is an ACT OF KINDNESS to reply in a timely fashion.

## COOKING BUDGET

There are many ways to make Apples of Gold affordable (see budget ideas, page xx). It is so important to have the food and hospitality segment so don't skip it because of finances. Instead, make it affordable by being creative and using careful budgeting. The food budget can be helped in several ways:

- Serve six weeks of soups, salads and desserts.

- Serve a brunch dish using eggs.
- Have only a sampling of meat. For example, cut a whole chicken breast into 8 pieces. Be sure to explain to the women ahead of time that the meat today is jut a sampling. This is often done at cooking schools and is called a tasting. There must be enough other less expensive foods to accompany the meat.
- Use leftovers from one class to another. Freeze, then demonstrate a new recipe with the leftovers. For example, turn leftover pork tenderloin into salad or an appetizer.
- If you use fruits or vegetables in a table decorations one week, use them in a recipe the following week.

## DECORATING IDEAS

If you are using several different tables, you can also use several different table settings. If you do not have enough tablecloths, perhaps you can borrow some. Inexpensive fabric in checked gingham, or a colorful print from the bargain table at the fabric or craft store will make a beautiful table. Place mats are fine too. I have also used beautiful bed sheets purchased on sale to dress up my tables.

I like using cloth because it makes the women feel special. It also teaches them to treat their guests the same way. Remember that everything we do in Apples of Gold is a teaching/learning process.

Tablecloths are easy to make and can be quite inexpensive. Find fabric on sale and sew a cloth. For a long table, hems are the only necessity. Use drapery or upholstery fabric which is 54 inches wide. If you do not sew, use iron-on hem tape. It works great!

Round tablecloths are not difficult either if you get a pattern or good instructions from a fabric store. It will never matter what is under the table once the cloth covers it. My husband makes round tables for me with plywood cut to the diameter I want. He adds legs from any wood he has on hand and I have a wonderful, strong table. With a cloth made long enough to go to the floor, nobody knows about the hodge-podge underneath.

Add a smaller square tablecloth diagonally over a round cloth for a dramatic affect. Your round cloth can be in a solid color that can be used through various seasons with the smaller square cloth in a contrasting color or print design that goes with the theme.

Many classes prefer to use place cards. It is a good way to mix up the mentors and participants. If using place cards, make them as attractive as you can, perhaps with a gold stamped apple and calligraphy. The mentors can take a head count during the cooking hour, and then set the place cards at the tables. This helps ensure that there are not empty chairs at the tables if there is a woman absent that week. Keep a record of who is sitting with whom and be sure to change arrangements from week to week.

Centerpiece ideas can be beautiful and simple. Our dining room table in Florida is long. I purchased two inexpensive copper planters, filled them with beach sand, and put small shells on top. Then I added candles for a beautiful affect. The candles will not drip on the table and the sand holds them tightly even when using very tall candles.

Sometimes I tuck flowers from my yard in with the candles. You can purchase in bulk at craft stores the little water bottles that florists use for fresh flowers. The flowers are low and do not present a 'hedge' which guest must try to speak across.

Using the same little water holders, you can scatter flowers around your table. Cut your stems short and place a few in each container. Tie with a pretty ribbon and you have a 'movable feast' for the eyes as you place them around your place settings.

An elegant and fairly inexpensive floral arrangement can be made with lacy greens and just a few dainty white flowers, perhaps baby's breath or something similar. Simplicity can appear so elegant when combined with a lovely table cloth.

Another wonderful example is an asparagus vase made by taking a tall jar such as an olive jar, placing two heavy rubber bands around the jar. Tuck asparagus under the rubber bands with the heads of asparagus pointed up. Wrap all of the jar. Cover the rubber bands with a pretty ribbon. Add some pretty pink or yellow flowers from your yard and you have a stunning centerpiece you can eat the next day!

Here are some other centerpiece ideas:

- Stack bowls and platters of assorted sizes and colors with red, green, and yellow peppers.
- Place a whole cauliflower on a plate and garnish with herbs.
- Use red, yellow and green apples together or separate.
- Spray apples gold and a pot silver for our theme verse
- Use a pretty dish, such as Gram's tureen with green plant
- Decorate with fabric
- Sprigs of plants from yard in tall olive jars
- Candles
- Herbs
- Teapots with a few flowers, or even plain
- Italian bottles, pasta, bread, bottle of oils
- Bird cages

It's also fun to decorate to a theme. For the lesson on Purity, I love to set at least one table completely in white. I use a white tablecloth, white dishes and napkins, and white flowers. Having just one table set in white really sets it apart as a reminder of the importance of purity.

Another mentor, Jean put wedding pictures, albums, napkins, confetti and rings on the tables for the husband lesson. What a simple but memorable way to decorate!

For the lesson about children, prepare foods that can be used as decorations as well such as a crown cake, a frog made with pickles, animals made with fruit. Many magazines have wonderful ideas for decorations.

Jean also decorated tables with dolls for children. Beanie Babies, tops, balls, cars and trucks, and other toys, especially old ones, make colorful and fun reminders of the children in our lives.

Balloons are always a fun decoration. Make a balloon bouquet, keeping the balloons very small. Tie and wrap on skewers and tuck into inexpensive flowerpots. Be creative! There's no end to the possibilities and what a special treat to the eye for your women.

## OPTIONS, OPTIONS

There are as many variations as there are Apples of Gold classes. One

Apples of Gold mentor has a volunteer cookie baking class at her home
several times before Christmas. They make 4,000 cookies for the
annual church Christmas program. What a ministry! The story of
how this cookie ministry started is fascinating:

> **Every year this mentor's church brings cookies to the
> Christmas program at church. Our mentor noticed that
> each year fewer and fewer home baked cookies were
> brought. In her frustration over the lack of home baked
> cookies, she told her husband she was going to stop
> bringing her homemade cookies as well.**
>
> **He said, "I have a better idea. You should bring all
> 4,000 cookies."**
>
> **This precious lady began having cookie baking days at
> her home weeks before Christmas. She taught the vol-
> unteers how to make her delicious and very special dec-
> orated cookies. No tastes were allowed, every cookie is
> counted, and carefully tucked into boxes for freezing. At
> the Christmas program every year now, all cookies are
> home baked!**
>
> **Isn't that just an incredible story?**

I sometimes hold a Tuesday class at my home. Here is a brief run-down
of my schedule:

- Choose menu and print recipes Friday or Saturday before class
- Set tables over weekend if possible. You might ask mentors, or
  another creative friend who wishes to help but cannot be a mentor, to come to your home and creatively set your tables. They
  may think of using your dishes in a fresh new way.

  We set tables for 4-6 women including a mentor to guide Table
  Talk questions. I believe smaller groups have better conversation and the women are more likely to share. Be sure that a place
  is reserved for a mentor by placing a name card, "mentor". Ideas
  for table settings are found later in this section.

- Monday Morning—groceries. Shop only for class, keep receipts for reimbursement. Or, ask someone to shop for you. Give a complete list.
- Place some large plastic trays on the counter.
- Sort all groceries onto trays according to recipes. Leave all ingredients out, so you do not have double work of putting them in cabinets and then finding them again.

    Prep refrigerated items. Mark on recipe all ref. Items, so that you don't forget them on morning of class. I print out recipe and put the recipe on the tray.
- Begin to prep foods in orderly fashion so nothing is skipped. Keep good notes on recipe to remind you of tasks completed and those to be done later. Measure ingredients into small custard cups or any small bowls. Cover with plastic wrap and keep on trays with recipe.

Why not try a garden picnic for one class. My friend, Karen, has one of the loveliest gardens I have seen. We once had our class in her garden. I prepared a box lunch for each participant. I found some nice white gift boxes, lined them with colorful tissue paper and filled them with goodies. At the wholesale food store I found some small containers with lids into which I put Greek Ravioli Salad. Sandwiches were wrapped in colorful plastic wrap.

I just opened my trunk and everyone picked a box. Karen gave a little tour of her garden, we ate our lunch and then had our Bible lesson. It was a special day.

A picnic lunch could also be served with pretty baskets or by wrapping lunch in a bandana or piece of pretty fabric, tied with a plaid ribbon.

Share family traditions or start new ones with the women in your group. My friend, Jacquie, who started Apples of Gold in her neighborhood in the Minneapolis area, purchased a piece of heavy muslin fabric. She made a tablecloth for her dining room table from the cloth. On special holidays, Thanksgiving and Christmas, her children write a special memory from the year with fabric pens. Jacquie then embroiders the writing and a heart around each. There are records of engagements, weddings, births and other special memories to remind everyone in the family of fun times together and the Lord's blessings.

Another variation of that idea is to use quilt squares. Some classes make a quilt with each participant preparing one square. When it is finished, it is hung at the church.

Another class suggests that a different mentor provides the centerpieces for the week she facilitates her lesson.

The ideas are endless. Be creative or find a creative friend to help you.

# CHAPTER 5

# The Celebration Dinner

## WHY CELEBRATE?

Every woman who becomes involved in Apples of Gold in a positive way is an asset to the program and to the church at large. Please do not skip having the celebration dinner. It really is the wrap-up for the program. Make it as lovely as you can and ask for help with setup and food as needed.

The celebration dinner is held after the six-week program is complete. Each woman invites her husband or a friend if she is single. This is a very special evening. We begin talking about it on the first week of class so that the women can plan for it.

It is important to establish the date of the dinner with the class present. I like to submit a couple of dates the first or second week. By the third week, we establish the date. Babysitters are lined up, Applesauce helpers are signed up, and the excitement builds up!

Plan the expenses for the dinner into your budget from the beginning. In many classes, mentors are eager to bring a donated dish to help with expenses. It is also a great help to the hostess and main cook.

Let everyone know ahead of time what the dress is for the evening and be specific. If this is an occasion where the women are expected to wear a dress or dressy pant outfit, and the men are expected to wear a jacket, everyone needs to understand that expectation. It is uncomfortable to be the only one in shorts!

The style of dress that is appropriate will vary from class to class and city to city. If your dinner is casual or a theme party, make that clear as well. We want each person to be comfortable. When a person is comfortable, they will have a more enjoyable time. When we are not thinking about how we look, we can concentrate more on others.

Explain to everyone the last week of class that there will be a time of sharing after dinner. That gives them a week or so to think about how Apples of Gold has affected their home and whether or not they want to share.

It is lovely to have music during dinner. Perhaps you know someone who will volunteer to play the piano. If using CD's, select well ahead of time. It is an easy thing to forget and you will not have time at the last minute. Select music that is good background music and not a distraction.

## SETTING THE TABLES

Plan ahead! Have a sign up sheet at the last class so that you have an exact count. You will have several tables to set for the dinner. You may have to borrow a table from a friend. Large folding tables work just fine.

I often set tables in front of my sofa or loveseat and place chairs around. The couples seem to enjoy the coziness of that arrangement. Several of my friends have set one of the tables up in a bedroom. That table is also quickly taken. There is a sense of surprise that is appealing to the couples.

If you will need to borrow some dishes or silverware, be sure to count how many of each item you have borrowed, so it is properly returned. Have tablecloths, napkins, dishes, glassware and serving items ready well in advance of the day.

Set the tables at least a day ahead, two or three days is better. Keep the day of the dinner strictly for food preparation and allow time for yourself! If you are sure that the tables are ready, you can forget about them completely until you light the candles.

Be sure to use cloth linens for this dinner. The tables do not have to match, but can be uniquely different. The guests will check out each table for ideas to use at home. In some classes, each mentor is responsible for the setting and decorating of one table. This is helpful to the hostess and will give a variety of ideas.

## WHAT TO EXPECT

Each Celebration Dinner is unique. The mentors for each class should meet and discuss the expectations for your class dinner. Decide on the menu and whether dinner will be served to each guest at the tables or buffet style.

I personally like serving the dinner at the table for several reasons. Learning to serve others is part of Apples of Gold. Treating our guests in this special way encourages them to desire to share that experience in their own homes.

How they enjoy having their contemporaries from previous classes wait on them. Sometimes they even become "difficult guests" just for fun!

I also believe serving the dinner is easier because it is orderly. It is much easier to control the timing of each course and to serve each course when ready. That, to me, is a "stress buster".

If you decide to share the responsibility of preparing food, it is important that you still stick to a prepared menu. Appetizers can have variety, but it if two women are preparing salad, each should prepare the same recipe. Have only three or four items for the dinner course, and the same dessert for everyone.

If you do decide on a buffet style meal, the same idea applies. Having one salad, one platter of meat, potatoes and one vegetable keeps the line moving. Remember you are feeding a large number of people. When each person has to make a choice between two different kinds of salad, potato, and meat, the line is slowed down considerably.

By planning the menu and assigning specific recipes for a potluck buffet, you are assured that each plate will look beautiful and will have contrasting colors and textures.

Another option is to prepare the meal together in one home on the day of the dinner. "Polished Apples" may also volunteer to help with the setting of tables and preparation of food. It is so wonderful to interact with these young women, with whom you have shared food and fellowship in previous classes.

If your budget is small, it is perfectly fine to minimize your menu. In some years, we asked the participants to bring appetizers. That is okay to do.

You can serve a less expensive cut of meat or even a wonderful casserole, salad, bread and dessert. Again, I would be sure that everyone was eating the same salad, casserole and dessert.

## COOKING THE DINNER

If you are the hostess and you are also cooking for the dinner in your home, you will need a good schedule. This schedule applies whether you are cooking alone or if others are helping you.

We usually have our Celebration Dinner on Friday night. Early in the week, I make sure the house is ready. My wonderful husband, washes windows and cleans off the walks around the house.

Have a checklist for the things you will need for the dinner.

- Number of tables and chairs needed.
- Check china, glassware and silverware
- Is everything spot-free and shining?
- Tablecloths cleaned and pressed
- Wednesday. Set tables.
- Plenty of clean dishcloths and towels for helpers ready to go.
- Aprons for dishwashers.

## A TYPICAL SCHEDULE FOR FOOD PREPARATION

I prepare the menu and print off the recipes a week before the dinner. From that menu I prepare my shopping list. Our menu consists of punch and appetizers served on the patio, a light soup, arranged or tossed salad, main course of meat, potatoes and vegetables with garnish, rolls with butter, dessert served with coffee and tea.

I do not cook until Thursday and Friday, so it is crucial that the house is completely ready!

On Thursday morning early, I shop for food. Just as I do for cooking class, I leave everything out that is not perishable. I arrange the recipes for the evening in order on my island and put the food items including seasonings on that recipe on a tray.

Choose just two appetizers that are easy to make and can be prepared on Thursday and made ready to serve on Friday. Often mentors will bring the appetizers ready to serve on a beautiful tray.

Punch can be mixed ahead and placed on punch bowl. Add the ice just before the guests are due to arrive.

I do not make the soup until Friday because the large stockpot I will need will not fit into my refrigerator. By making the soup, Friday afternoon, it can simmer until needed. I have made soups that freeze well, another big time saver.

Prepare all the ingredients for the soup so the soup can be made quickly and easily. Do not prepare a complicated soup. This year I made Artichoke Soup and it was a big hit. Chop onions, lettuce, parsley, etc. I did need to puree this soup, so I allowed a few extra minutes late in the day to do that.

Wash all salad ingredients, chop onions, cucumbers, tomatoes, or whatever needs to be cut. Store in plastic storage bags in refrigerator until ready. Make dressing early in the day, store in large glass jars. With this method, it takes only a few minutes to prepare salad for 30-40 people.

I usually serve green beans that mentors or helpers (and sometimes their husbands) have cleaned for me the night before. I wash them and place them in a large cooking pot. All I have to do the night of the dinner is turn the stove on at the time on my schedule.

Prepare potatoes or rice as much ahead of time as possible.

The timing of the meat is crucial. If your meat needs to cook several hours, make sure it is done well ahead of time. It can just rest in a slow oven.

Plug in the coffeepot about an hour ahead of time. Fill sugar bowls early, have cream pitchers ready. Servers can quickly add cream just before serving.

Have kettle of hot water ready to go on stove for those who prefer hot tea. Have plenty of ice for ice water and pitchers ready to fill.

## SERVING THE DINNER

After you have graduated your first class, the "Polished Apples" will be your assistants and servers. For your first class, ask some beloved, fun loving friends, both men and women, from church to help. We love to have husband and wife teams serving, and they love working together. They remember how much the dinner meant to them and are eager to help serve!

> **After one of the dinners, one of the new class members came into the kitchen after the dinner and said, "Wow, next year I can help serve!"**
> **One of the servers replied, "Only if I am sick!**

One particular friend, Dave, has served all but one or two of our dinners and does a superb job. He has also served as kitchen manager for the dinner. Many of the servers have served for several years. It is so much fun having them in the kitchen with me. They are all well qualified to serve and serve with a joyful spirit. It is a good idea to have some seasoned help along with new helpers.

My husband and I can truly enjoy our guests because of the willing and expert helpers in the kitchen.

If possible, have the servers wear a dark skirt or trousers, and a white shirt. Take a photo of them when they arrive and when they leave. We have some great and memorable shots!

I ask all the helpers to arrive 30 minutes early and give very clear instructions for the evening. Write out a schedule for them that they can follow. This allows the mentors and their spouses to be a part of the party, and not consumed with the serving. If possible, assign a manager for the evening. This person will check on the progress of the dinner, and read the checklist to be sure everything is done.

Prepare a time schedule for the evening as well and stick to it. It is important that promises to babysitters are kept and that everyone can stay to the very end. The sharing time after dinner is as important as the dinner itself.

You will need at least three couples or six helpers for a dinner of 35-

40 guests. Show them the schedule and ask them what part they want to handle.

This is a typical schedule for the servers at our dinner in Holland.

Helpers arrive at 6 PM. Thank everyone for helping. Tell them how terrific they look and how much you appreciate their willingness to work. BE SURE THE SERVING STAFF HAS FUN!

I like to tell about the menu for the night and how I would like it to be served. Remind everyone to serve from the left and remove from the right. It is important to also be clear about which dishes stay on the table and which are removed for the different courses.

Time Table:

- 6:30   Guests arrive, are greeted by a mentoring couple and given nametags.
- 6:30   Serve punch and appetizers (2 people)
- 6:45   Light candles and fill water glasses (2 people)
- 6:50   Fill soup bowls. I serve a cream soup that is easy to pour. We use pitchers for serving the soup.
- 6:50   Guests are assembled for prayer. My husband welcomes everyone to our home and gives simple instructions for seating. He offers prayer of thanks for the food, and for our spouses and mentors. When guests arrive at their seat, their soup course is already set before them. Meanwhile, in the kitchen, salad is assembled on plates
- 7:15   Soup bowls are cleared and salad is served. Water glasses checked. In the kitchen, a team is serving up the main course. One person serves the meat, another adds the potatoes, vegetables and garnish.

**At one of the Celebration Dinners, one of my ovens was not turned on properly and was cold! It was time to serve the dinner and the meat was raw. Time to panic! Not quite! We asked everyone to eat the salad course leisurely, turned the oven on 500 degrees and waited it out. It was a good lesson for all!**

- 7:40    Salad dishes are cleared and dinner is served. Dinner rolls are passed to each person. The kitchen team is serving up dessert. We often quickly wash the salad plates and re-use them for dessert. This works very well.
- 8:10    Remove dinner plates and bread plates, if they are used. Serve dessert, coffee and tea.

During the entire dinner, there are teams washing dishes. It is a good idea to switch throughout the evening so that every person has the opportunity to mingle with the guests.

Again, it is important to give very specific instructions about the dish-washing. It is truly faster to hand wash and dry as you go. If using the electric dishwasher, be clear as to which dishes can be safely washed in the dishwasher. Teach dishwashers to change dishwater often and to use only the cleanest towels.

It is easy to loose utensils on a night like this. I ask the helpers to put all the silver into a bucket filled with warm, soapy water before scrap-ing the plate. It keeps silver from accidentally slipping off plate into the garbage.

Be sure there is enough dinner for all the servers. They can eat between courses, or after dinner is served to the guests. There is a win-dow of about 20 minutes while guest are eating main course for them to eat a bit.

Take many photos of the dinner and throughout the six weeks of class. Put them in an album. Take a photo of each table, so the next time you will know exactly what you did before, either to copy or to make sure it is different. Be sure to take a group photo of each class as well.

## FOOD FOR THE SOUL

After dinner, let everyone stretch their legs a bit since they have been sitting a while. Tell your guests where the restrooms are located. They ask everyone to gather in the living room or family room and to make themselves comfortable. Begin by singing a few choruses if possible. Sing either with or without accompaniment. Ask for favorite songs from the guests

Begin to share. This may come slowly at first; be patient. Often a mentor will start the sharing by telling the younger women what a joy the class has been to her. Often husbands will choose to share what Apples of Gold has meant to their wife and to their marriage and family.

Ask the host or another mentor's husband to share specifically to the men about encouraging their wives in what has been taught and to use the gifts God has given her. Give instruction to the men about their responsibility to love their wives according to scripture. It is an effective time. The following is a testimony from Clare De Graaf husband of Apples of gold mentor Susan De Graaf of Calvary Church, Grand Rapids, Michigan and the Celebration Dinner address he delivered:

**For the past six weeks a dozen young women and their mentors have been meeting at our house. My wife, Susan, was the weekly mentor. The Apples of Gold program culminates with a dinner with all the women, including the mentors, along with their husbands, or significant others. This is an incredible opportunity for the men to finally meet the women their wives have been describing. I've not met their husbands but for the past several years the teaching mentors have gotten indications from each group of women that some of the husbands are either not believers or very immature Christians.**

**After a wonderful dinner served by the cooking mentors and their helpers and spouses, everyone gathered in our living room and for the first time I saw all the men, for whom I'd been praying. Some of the men feel obviously out of place either because they are socially awkward, don't know any of the other men, or are nervous being around men and women who are obviously in love with Jesus. Maryanne, the lead mentor, opened by introducing all the mentors and cooking mentors. After we sang a few praise songs she turned the meeting over to me.**

**I began by thanking the cooking mentors and the teaching mentors and giving my wife, Susan, who was the cook-**

ing mentor, a dozen roses. I felt that gesture was important for several reasons. First, I wanted to tell Susan how
much I appreciated all the work and time she's put into
this ministry. Secondly, I wanted to honor her in front of
everyone present as someone I cherish. And thirdly, I
wanted to give some of the men present some practical
ideas on how a Christina man honors his wife, not just
for her accomplishments, but for her character.

Finally, it was time for me to address the group, but in
particular the men.

"Every woman in this room has spent the last six weeks
learning to be godly women. I've been given fifteen minutes to flog you men into being passable husbands.
Frankly, I'd have a better shot at parting the Red Sea, I
said with a laugh." I think it's important for people to feel
comfortable and laughter is a great way to set people's
mind at ease.

I began reading from page 40 in the *Apples of Gold* book:

"Once a pastor was telling a children's sermon. He
asked, 'What's gray and furry and hops about in the for-
est?' A boy tentatively raised his hand to say, "I know the
answer if Jesus, but it sure sounds like a squirrel to me!"

In the same way, it's easy to guess the "right" answer to
the following question, but what is the "real" answer?
Here's the question: How would you order these relationships in your life?

GOD        CHILDREN        HUSBAND

Though the "real" answer is often Children, Husband,
God, the "right answer" is God, Husband, Children. Your
relationship with God must be the most important relationship in your life. Everything you do hinges on this relationship—the decisions you make, the reactions you
have to circumstances, the way you relate to others,
your sense of joy and peace. Everything! Your relationship
with God is for time and eternity."

I then quoted from Peter Drucker, an internationally known management guru. The key to one of his endearing principles is, "Above all else, do the first things first!"

"I'd like to talk to you men tonight about getting first things first. I'm more than qualified to speak on this subject because for the first 30 years of my life I didn't. Frankly, 20 years ago I wouldn't have been caught dead standing up in front of a group of men saying the kinds of things I want to talk to you about tonight.

"On the personal side, in 1979, Susan and I had been married 11 years. We had three children and I was a good father and an OK husband. You see, the kids were small and it was fun just being their daddy, but marriage was work. There seemed to be no end to the management decisions we had to make that often robbed us from just enjoying each other.

"On the business side of things, I owned a small company that manufactured parts for the office furniture industry. We had approximately 12 million annual in sales, 174 employees, no long-term debt, a summer home on Lake Michigan, and a Mercedes in the garage. From every human perspective I had it make. The truth of the matter was that my business was my mistress. It was where I really found my identity.

"On the spiritual side, we attended church regularly, I believed Jesus Christ to be the Son of God, I believed the Bible was true, we gave regularly to the church, I served as a deacon, Sunday school teacher and on the evangelism committee. I enjoyed the church culture and the people. Spiritually, I bought the whole 'party line'. However, the truth was that Christianity was basically a Sunday thing. It simply wasn't personal to me.

"At 30 years of age, I was on top of the world. Then one day in the shower I felt a lump in my neck. Several weeks later a doctor walked into my hospital room and

told me I had lymphoma cancer and only five to nine years
to live. I remember one of the first thoughts that struck
me – what difference does it make that I made 13.2% on
sales.

"God used cancer to shake me and bring me to my sens-
es. Within weeks a lawyer from our church invited me to
a small Bible study in a local restaurant. At first glance
I looked at the materials and it looked like Christianity
101. The study material asked questions like, "How to be
sure you are a Christian", "Who is Jesus Christ" and "How
to Experience God's Love and Forgiveness." But as I
began to study week after week, looking up the passages in scripture, I was saddened to realize how little I
knew about what Christ truly taught and expected from
His followers.

"I had always accepted Christ as my Savior, but I just
wasn't ready to surrender my life to Him. I didn't want
to become a Jesus freak, I didn't want to have to sell my
Mercedes or go of to Nigeria to be a missionary. The
truth is I simply didn't want to surrender control of my
life to Jesus Christ. So for nearly six months, I read the
Bible, prayed, talked with other godly men and grew in
my understanding of what God requires of me because of
what Christ did for me. I was really wrestling with God
and He with me.

"Finally, one February morning, having been up for several hours, sitting in my living room crying, I finally did
business with Jesus Christ. I said to Him, "Jesus, I know
that I am a sinner, I'm not just a sinner because I do selfish or bad things, but because by nature I've been in rebellion against you and separated from the Father. I'm
sorry. I want to be done with all of that and I ask forgiveness for my selfishness, my foul mouth, my rebellion
and my pride. I believe you are the Son of God, that you
came to earth to die on the cross for me, that you rose

again from the dead and there is no other way or me to ever be right with the Father other than accepting your offer of salvation. Thank you for loving me even when I didn't love you. Thank you for seeking me out even when I wasn't looking for you. I surrender every area of my life to you.

"I finished that prayer and I wasn't quite sure what to expect. There were no bright lights or voices from God but I knew something had happened inside of me because within days I became exceptionally sensitized to sin areas of my life. For the first time in my life I wanted to overcome them, not because I feared God, but because I loved Jesus. I knew that if I was going to be a visible, vocal and sincere follower of Jesus, my filthy language and dirty jokes had no place in my life.

"I also noticed that the Holy Spirit began changing the desires of my heart. He deepened my concern for other people and gave me a heart for the lost. He gave me a heightened thirst for Biblical truth. Christ deepened my love for my wife and my children and heightened my desire to be a godly husband and father. I need to be honest with you. I'm still very much a work in process. I still wrestle with pride, materialism and pure thoughts and motives. But, the goal of my life is to be a godly man.

"Enough about me. What about you? Would the people who know you best, your wife, your children, and the people you work with or play golf with – would they consider you to be a godly man? If so, I praise God for you. If not, have you considered why not? Do you even want to be? I'd love to help you on that journey. Please give me a call this week and let me help you as others have helped me. Trust me! Once Christ is number one in your life and you truly get first things first, it will transform every area of your life.

"Your wives have just finished six weeks of study. How

can we husbands leverage this experience to help our
wives and how can you, as couples grow closer? I have just
five ideas and then I'm done:

1)  Honor her with your time and attention.

    a) Have you spent any serious time reading the
    Apples of Gold material?

    b) Take her to dinner or sit in front of the fire and
    ask her, 'What have you learned and how can I help
    you"?

    c) Here's a bit hint! Don't make a single suggestion,
    just ask questions and affirm her. Don't try to fix it!
    (By the way , if you follow that one piece of advice,
    it may save you thousands of dollars in counseling
    later on in life.)

2)  Honor her by becoming a student of your wife's heart.

        Susan would often say, 'This is what I'm feeling', and
    I would respond, 'That's not logical. That doesn't
    make sense to me.' In my mind, emotions were some
    sort of second d class logic. However, after watching
    just how often her feelings were more accurate in
    assessing many situations that my acts, I began to
    appreciate her wisdom more. Listen to your wife's feel-
    ings. What is she really saying? Learn from her.

3)  Discuss ways you as a couple and each of you per-
    sonally, could grow spiritually and relationally.

    a) Perhaps there are friends who are hindering your
    spiritual growth.

    b) Should you be in a couples Bible study, or group?

    c) How could you use your home to reach out to oth-
    ers?

    d) Are there some bad habits in your life that are
    sending mixed signals to your children?

    e) Should you read some books together, or attend
    a seminar or conference on marriage?

4)  Commit yourself to a time of daily Bible reading and

prayer.

a)  The truth of the matter is, most women are more spiritually mature than their husbands are. It's also truth that most men are content to have their wives be more spiritually mature, but that's unacceptable to God. You will never be the spiritual leader of your home unless you are committed to knowing God's word and living it out on a consistent basis.

b)  If you don't know where to begin, I'd suggest beginning with the (book) of Matthew and reading straight through the New Testament.

c)  If you've never really had a regular time of Bible study and prayer, I'd suggest contacting the most spiritually mature man you know and ask for some help. Or again, give me a call, I'd love to help you form some good spiritual habits.

5)  If you want spiritually and emotionally healthy children, love your wives. One of the first books I ever read as a Christian was, "What Wives Wish Their Husbands Knew About Women" by Jim Dobson. My wife and I would like to have each man have a copy of this book tonight as our gift to you.

"On behalf of all the men, we thank you, our wives, and honor you for your investment in yourself and in our families. We praise God for you."

And then I closed with prayer.

When the meeting broke up, the next half hour became very important as individual men and women came up to me. Several men let it be know that they needed help. I think it's extremely important that the person who speaks be available to the men, or agrees to network them with other spiritually mature men. I've met many men who would say months later, "Oh, I meant to call you, but I just never got around to do it". If you sense there is an

**interest, make an appointment right on the spot to meet with a man.**

**For a number of months following that night, I prayed for the men and women who were present. While Apples of Gold's primary ministry is to women, the number one dream of every married Christian woman is a godly husband. A house divided against itself cannot stand.**

Before closing for the night, enjoy a time of shared prayer. We have a tradition of singing and signing the chorus, *Jesus We Crown You with Praise* at the close.

> *Jesus, we crown You with praise.*
> *Jesus, we crown You with praise.*
> *We love and adore You*
> *Bow down before You*
> *Jesus, we crown You with praise.*

Then everyone is free to leave or to linger. This summer as couples walked to the front door to leave, all the kitchen helpers were sitting and sharing in the family room. They had all the dishes washed and dried, and were cuddled up with their spouses. It was a lovely sight.

I cannot express enough my deep love and enjoyment of these young couples in my life. I know other mentors who feel just as I do. These precious souls are the next generation of the church. They are the ones who will nurture and nourish the generation who follow after them. How important it is that we obey God and do our part. What a blessing!

# CHAPTER 6

# *What's Next?*

## APPLESAUCE—A WONDERFUL BLEND

When class is over, a common comment is "I don't want this to end" or "I flunked the course and need to return". The fact is that six weeks gives the participants just a taste of this special relationship of mentor and friend. Applesauce is designed to help fill that gap, with meetings and events held from time to time.

Applesauce is a gathering of all the women who have attended one of your programs of Apples of Gold. Obviously, this number will grow with each additional class and you will need to find creative ways to host the women.

Ideally, Applesauce could meet monthly or bi-monthly. You could continue Applesauce with each class separately, but our local class has really benefited from meeting with *all* the women. This is truly a wonderful time of fellowship and joy.

The truth is, Applesauce needs more attention than we have given it. At a recent meeting in my home, we surveyed the women about Applesauce. Ideas surfaced such as more events with husbands, topical studies, question and answer sessions and yes, even the suggestion of a sleepover. This could actually be a terrific opportunity to chat long into the night about many different issues facing these younger women.

Here are just a few ideas that have actually been use by Apples of Gold groups:

## SPRING LUNCHEON

We have held a luncheon in Holland each year in May. One of our mentors has the perfect home for such an event and has graciously hosted us year after year. The mentors bring salad, breads, and dessert. Mary sets the tables beautifully and creatively.

One year we had a hat contest. There were prizes for the most beautiful, most creative, etc. It was lovely to see all the women in hats. We have wonderful photos of that day. The most creative hat was a colander decorated with kitchen utensils hanging down. It was indeed the center of attention.

Each year we have a speaker after lunch. One friend came to talk about encouragement, another brought a basic clothing wardrobe. She dressed the young women in a variety of outfits and accessories. It was both fun and helpful.

## CHRISTMAS COFFEE

This Christmas we had a coffee on a Tuesday morning. After enjoying our coffee and goodies, we had a time of sharing, singing, and praying for one another. Each woman brought homemade cookies to the event. We purchased pretty white boxes, decorated them with a cutout of a gold apple, wrote Merry Christmas from Apples of Gold in gold pen, and tagged each box with a scripture blessing. We called them Blessing Baskets.

The church gave us a list of shut-ins and widows. Each woman packed a lovely box of cookies, picked a name from the list, and took her family to visit the shut-ins. We suggested that perhaps the children could sing a Christmas carol or two for the person they visit. We have already heard wonderful stories of the joy that act of service brought to the recipients of the basket.

Serving others brings great joy to the one serving and the recipient. This idea also brings the generations together, a goal of Apples of Gold.

## TOPICAL STUDIES

Many groups like to continue to meet together using topical studies available. Integrity, Honesty, Fairness, Friendship, and Discipline are good subjects to address with your group. I am writing lessons I call CORE VALUES about some of these topics. We plan to publish them as additional study resources for your Apples of Gold women.

## APPLESEEDS AND APPLE BLOSSOMS

One Applesauce friend has started a Bible study with her daughter and her friends. She has creatively planned social events that include the friends' mothers as well. These teens are growing very strong in Christ and have set an example in their school. They also plan service projects to minister to those in need. It was such an inspiring time for the Applesauce women.

Soon Apples of Gold will have a study for girls age 9-12 called *Appleseeds*. The focus is on teaching the girls their value as a child of God. We are also looking at a study for teen girls called Apple Blossoms. This is a wonderful opportunity to extend the mentoring experience while reaching young women during their formative years.

Ask your classes what they would like to do after Apples of Gold is over. You will receive plenty of ideas, I promise! The important thing is to keep being involved with these women, letting them know that you care, and that you are available to them.

I know the great creativity that exists among the Apples of Gold mentors. You will come up with your own wonderful ideas for Applesauce. What an inspiration some of your ideas have been to me!

## APPLES OF GOLD AS AN OUTREACH

What started as a ministry within my own church has now spread across the country and around the world. I believe that part of the success of Apples of Gold is that it is reaching out to women who feel that something is missing in their lives. The Focus on the Family broadcasts have brought many inquiries from women who are not involved in a church or who are new in their town, or are looking for a way to make some new friends.

Though Apples of Gold has been largely used as a program to encourage young Christian women, I believe it could be used as an outreach to women with little or no church background. I receive many letters from women in new and growing churches who are interested in using Apples of Gold to reach out to their community. Sometimes people visit a new church and don't really connect with others right away. Apples of Gold could offer the gift of friendship in an environment of joy and laughter.

Inviting a new neighbor or someone who has just visited your church a few times to a class in a home may be just the thing that will reach her heart. Having fun together in someone's kitchen, meeting new friends over a cup of coffee, may feel more like a safe harbor. Learning about the Bible in a home with just a few women may open the heart to discussion. In the study time, a woman will learn that other women have deep heart needs much like her own. At the table she will have the opportunity to share Table Talk ideas with others, and benefit from the experience of the mentors.

What a warm environment in which to learn about God and the Bible. Look around your neighborhood—your church. You may be standing in a rich orchard ripe and ready to harvest. In days gone by, neighbor knew each other well and shared coffee and a chat. Today, many of us do not know our neighbor's names. As you probably know by now, I believe our homes are precious treasures given to us by our Heavenly Father, to be used to glorify Him. Opening your home to new friends and neighbors may be just the way God will use you to bring them in to His kingdom.

Why not plan your Apples of Gold group around the assumption that there will be new, unexpected guests invited? Order an extra book or two, set an extra place setting, add a few more veggies to the pot...It may not feel comfortable at first but what a blessing outreach can be! It is God's plan that we reach out to other too share the Good News that we treasure. Go for it!

## FINAL WORDS

It is my sincere prayer that you will find many ways to perpetuate the blessing of Apples of Gold in your life, in your church, and in your community. There are thousands of needy women longing for your presence in their lives.

Thank you so much for serving Jesus in this loving and obedient way, for the changes you are making in the church of Christ, and in the families you are serving. I pray for you often and love hearing from you with ideas from your classes and testimonies of God's grace. God bless each of you as you seek to serve Him in obedience and love.

Please write me at **www.applesofgold.org** with testimonies and suggestions. It is an effective way for us to communicate around the world. Check the website from time to time for new ideas, my travel schedule, and testimonies from the classes and recipes.

renewing the heart®
*Truth and Grace for Daily Living*

## Welcome to a Special Place Just for Women

We hope you've enjoyed this book.
Renewing the Heart, a ministry of Focus on the Family,
is dedicated to equipping and encouraging women in all facets of their
lives. Through our weekly call-in radio program, our Web site, and a
variety of other outreaches, Renewing the Heart is a place to find
answers, gain support, and, most of all, know you're among friends.

## How to Reach Us

For more information and additional resources, visit our Web site at
www.renewingtheheart.com. Here, you'll find articles, devotions, and
broadcast information on our weekly call-in radio program,
"Renewing the Heart," hosted by Janet Parshall.

To request any of these resources, call Focus on the Family at
800-A-FAMILY (800-232-6459). In Canada, call 800-661-9800.

You may also write us at:
Focus on the Family, Colorado Springs, CO 80995

In Canada, write to: Focus on the Family,
P.O. Box 9800, Stn. Terminal, Vancouver, B.C. V6B 4G3

To learn more about Focus on the Family or to find out if we have an
associate office in your country, please visit www.family.org.

We'd love to hear from you!

## About the Author

Betty Huizenga began the *Apples of Gold* seminars in her home many years ago, and now other women are duplicating the seminars around the country. After she and her husband retired, Betty felt the Lord calling her to minister to younger women. She and her husband now divide their time between Michigan and Florida.

# Apples of Gold

The life-changing principles of Betty's seminars come to life in book form, offering women an encouraging plan for developing kindness, purity, hospitality, and love for their children and husband. ISBN: 0-78143-352-5

# Appleseeds

Divided into several classes filled with fun projects and fellowship, this book helps young women develop godly self-esteem, social skills that can be used to disciple others, and Christian characteristics such as honesty, integrity, and servanthood. Both the girls who participate in the program and the mothers who volunteer to facilitate will be reminded of their value to God, themselves, and the Body of Christ. ISBN: 0-78143-805-5